Sustainable Finance

Sustainable Finance is a concise and authoritative reference series linking research and practice. It provides reliable concepts and research findings in the ever growing field of sustainable investing and finance, SDG economics and Leadership with the declared commitment to present the theories, methods, tools and investment approaches that can fulfil the United Nations Sustainable Development Goals and the Paris Agreement COP 21/22 alongside with de-risking assets and creating triple purpose solutions that ensure the parity of profit, people and planet through choice architecture passion and performance. The series addresses market failure, systemic risk and reinvents portfolio theory, portfolio engineering as well as behavioural finance, financial mediation, product innovation, shared values, community building, business strategy and innovation, exponential tech and creation of social capital. Sustainable Finance and SDG Economics series helps to understand keynotes on international guidelines, guiding accounting and accountability principles, prototyping new developments in triple bottom line investing, cost benefit analysis, integrated financial first plus impact first concepts and impact measurement. Going beyond adjacent fields (like accounting, marketing, strategy, risk management) it integrates the concept of psychology, innovation, exponential tech, choice architecture, alternative economics, blue economy shared values, professions of the future, leadership, human and community development, team culture, impact, quantitative and qualitative measurement, Harvard Negotiation, mediation and complementary currency design using exponential tech and ledger technology. Books in the series contain latest findings from research, concepts for implementation, as well as best practices and case studies for the finance industry.

More information about this series at http://www.springer.com/series/15807

Harald Bolsinger • Johannes Hoffmann •
Bernd Villhauer
Editors

The European Central Bank as a Sustainability Role Model

Philosophical, Ethical and Economic Perspectives

Springer

Editors
Harald Bolsinger
FHWS University of Applied Sciences
Würzburg-Schweinfurt
Würzburg, Germany

Johannes Hoffmann
Goethe University Frankfurt/Main
Frankfurt/Main, Germany

Bernd Villhauer
Weltethos-Institut at the University of
Tübingen
Tübingen, Germany

ISSN 2522-8285 ISSN 2522-8293 (electronic)
Sustainable Finance
ISBN 978-3-030-55449-1 ISBN 978-3-030-55450-7 (eBook)
https://doi.org/10.1007/978-3-030-55450-7

This Springer imprint is published by the registered company Springer Nature Switzerland AG.
The registered company address is: Gewerbestrasse 11, 6330 Cham, Switzerland

Preface

While economists argue about whether the new ECB head Christine Lagarde should continue the relaxed monetary policy of her predecessor Mario Draghi in the interest of financial stability and in the direction of 2% inflation, the Research Group Wirtschaft und Finanzen (Economics and Finance) of the Weltethos-Institut at the University of Tübingen is pushing forward the question of whether the ECB is failing completely regarding this very issue in the interest of environmental, social, and cultural sustainability.

The expert panel meeting on October 29, 2019, at Goethe University was preceded by Petition 429/2017 submitted by economic ethicist Harald Bolsinger to the Committee on Petitions of the EU Parliament. This petition highlights the ECB's active participation in undermining the values of the Charter of Fundamental Rights (i.e., via its portfolio policy) which is binding for all EU institutions.

With this conference, the Wirtschaft und Finanzen Research Group of the Weltethos-Institut at the University of Tübingen posed the important question of whether the ECB, as an EU institution, can act independently of the EU's human rights and sustainability principles. There is a risk that it may in fact fail to take such principles into account for economic reasons. Measured in terms of the volume of funds managed by the ECB, this makes the efforts of ethically sustainable investment virtually meaningless. However, sustainable investment is of great importance as a means of social and economic transformation.

This concern was discussed and made transparent in our expert panel discussion "A Sustainable Europe: The ECB as a cardinal mistake?" We also publicly pointed out the ECB's responsibility to adhere to the ethical and social principles of the EU in their economic policy implementation.

In this respect, the Frankfurt conference brought together philosophical, economic, legal, and political arguments which we present to a wider audience in this publication.

We have already been able to achieve a successful first step; on November 11, 2019 Harald Bolsinger spoke before the Committee on Petitions of the European Parliament. Parliamentarians praised the petition and resolved to pursue the matter. The demands are to be submitted to the new head of the ECB and discussed in the

Committee on Economic and Monetary Affairs of the EU Parliament as well as in other decision-making bodies.

The expert panel discussion was held in a place steeped in the history of Germany, namely the Eisenhower Hall of the Goethe University in Frankfurt. Designed by the architect Hans Poelzig on behalf of IG-Farben from 1928 to 1930, it is the most modern industrial office building of the twentieth century.

After the war, the Americans moved in and the building became their headquarters for the next 43 years. On July 1, 1948, the prime ministers of the various German states were called upon to draft the Basic Law for the Federal Republic of Germany in this very room. Therefore, the IG Farben House can be seen as the birthplace of our German Constitution. The negotiations regarding the introduction of the new currency, the Deutsche Mark, were also conducted here, inextricably linking this place with the Deutsche Mark forever.

In 1995, the Americans moved out, and the question of what to do with the building, or in other words who should move in, was posed. In negotiations between the Federal Government and the State of Hesse, two proposals were in the air, namely the ECB and the Goethe University.[1]

We chose this historic venue for our conference in the hope that it too will contribute to a better future—a truly sustainable Eurosystem...

P.S. On August 5, 2020, the Committee on Petitions of the European Parliament received a letter from the Directorate General International & European Relations of the European Central Bank. In this letter, it is set out that the ECB has the primary objective to ensure price stability over the medium term. Whether this can or should be done based on the human rights-related principles and obligations is discussed in the following way: the Directorate acknowledges that the ECB is an addressee of the Charter of Fundamental Rights, but "does not automatically have an obligation to enforce the Charter vis-à-vis the issuers of securities it considers eligible for use in its monetary policy operations." This raises a lot of questions not only for the ECB but for other EU bodies. The short letter, which tries to discuss the complicated matter on two pages, supplies material for further research in more than one perspective. For example one should take a closer look at this conclusion: "The ECB also cannot simply defer to the findings of private self-authenticated sources such as those proposed by the Petitioner." That is probably aiming at NGOs—but is it also true for credit rating agencies—and what would that mean for the analysis and the European investment policy? All this shows that the discussion about the rules and principles of the ECB strategy has only started...

Würzburg, Germany — Harald Bolsinger
Frankfurt/Main, Germany — Johannes Hoffmann
Tübingen, Germany — Bernd Villhauer

[1] Meißner, Werner/Rebentisch Dieter/Wang, Wilfried HG. Der Poelzig-Bau. From I.G. Farben-Haus zur Goetheuniversität, Frankfurt 1999.

Contents

Where Do We Stand When It Comes to Sustainable Financial Markets?

Johannes Hoffmann

Abstract If we intend to support sustainability in the financial markets, research and analysis must come first. In the last 30 years, the groundwork has been laid by the Ethical Environmental Research Group (Forschungsgruppe Ethisch-Ökologisches Rating) leading to a rating system for Impact Investing. The article shows the progress in Sustainable Finance through the years and highlights essential aspects, connecting environmental, social and cultural compatibility. Only an integrated view can lead the European fiscal and financial policy towards a new level.

1 Introduction

After 30 years of scientific work on the promotion of environmental, social and sustainable investments and through the common interest in the Ethical Environmental Rating Research Group, we are now well prepared for sustainable development within the framework of the market economy. The contribution of the Research Group was and is supported by the effort to expose hidden issues: Making the unseen visible, freeing people from outdated traditions, encouraging new ways, and accompanying and promoting effective altruists. Taking the path of "subversive integration," [1] so that human development can succeed in communion with creation. For the development of environmental, social, economic and intercultural sustainability in the market economy, it makes sense to recall the beginnings and to take a look at the current state of environmental, social and intercultural sustainability in the economy. This will certainly provide clues for consistent environmental and social action in business, finance and the fiscal system. This must be recognised, publicised politically and its political implementation promoted. For me, this means in concrete terms that the example of the ECB's de facto approach, the central financial management institution in Europe, must be used to promote this more effectively. That is the intention of this conference.

J. Hoffmann (✉)
Goethe University Frankfurt/Main, Frankfurt/Main, Germany
e-mail: j.hoffmann@em.uni-frankfurt.de

H. Bolsinger et al. (eds.), *The European Central Bank as a Sustainability Role Model*, Sustainable Finance, https://doi.org/10.1007/978-3-030-55450-7_1

2 Ethical Environmental Investments and their Origins

There were already attempts in the 1920s to integrate thinking around environmental, social and sustainability issues into the investment process. However, the economic and political possibilities of ethical money management were brought to the fore by two spectacular measures taken by ethically oriented investors. One was the successful boycott of Dow Chemical in the USA during the Vietnam War, due to the company's supply of napalm to the military. The second was the boycott of the apartheid regime in South Africa, which contributed decisively to the peaceful replacement of the regime. The experience of the political effectiveness of boycotts or divestment motivated ethically oriented investors to use financial investments not only as a means for individual spectacular actions but systematically for an ethical-environmental shaping of the financial market. This began in the USA and England as early as the 1980s. It is no coincidence that EIRIS is one of the oldest sustainability agencies, founded by Peter Webster [2] coming from a Quaker background.

In Germany the concept of responsible investment started to emerge in the 1990s. More and more investors recognized the ethical responsibility of their money. They no longer wanted the money to be used for weapons production, human rights abuses, environmental damage etc. The prerequisite for this was an instrument with which the environmental, social and cultural compatibility of companies and other asset classes could be evaluated.

In 1991, Christian-oriented bank managers and church institutions suggested to found the project group Ethical-Environmental Rating (EÖR) at the Department of Catholic Theology of the Goethe University for the development of such an evaluation instrument. A first result was the so-called Frankfurt-Hohenheimer Leitfaden (FHL) [3], an internationally recognised criteria tree, which was reflected in the Corporate Responsibility Rating (CRR) methodology of Oekom Research AG in Munich. The CRR is now firmly established. Oekom Research AG was able to expand its market position and last year entered into a merger with ISS in New York.

In a further step, the research group founded a consortium of ethically oriented investors, CRIC e.V., in 2000 as an information and investment platform [4]. Finally, with the participation of the research group, the Forum Nachhaltige Geldanlagen (Germany's representative in the Pan-European Sustainable Investment Forum EUROSIF) was founded in 2001, in which financial actors such as investment managers, asset owners and service providers can get involved. The FNG awards an annual label for the assessment of sustainability funds [5]. Developments in Germany, as in other countries, show that ethically motivated investors have given the impetus for the market segment of ethical investments, which they utilise.

The current state of development in Germany and Europe is a success story that began around the year 2000. Today, trillions are invested worldwide in a large number of funds with different ethical-environmental profiles. Globally, sustainable investing assets in the five major markets stood at $30.7 trillion at the start of 2018, a 34 percent increase in 2 years [6].

Finally, the status of the signatories of the UN Principles for Responsible Investment (UN PRI) should also be mentioned. "Since its launch in 2006, more than 2500 institutional investors have joined the initiative, managing a total investment volume of around USD 90 trillion (as of 12/2018)."

Sustainable investments are also proving particularly interesting for large institutional investors such as pension funds, insurance companies, etc. Experience in recent years has shown that long-term (10 years and longer) ethical-environmental investments in the real economy (green building, sustainable infrastructure and land and forestry [7]) generate exactly what these institutions need to fulfil their contractual obligations and at the same time promote sustainable real economy projects, with average returns above the inflation rate.

The signs for responsible investments are therefore good, first because numerous studies have shown that responsible investments are generally not inferior to traditional ones in terms of returns and are indeed helpful in terms of competitive positioning. "A study published by the Harvard Business School and the London School of Business comes to the conclusion that taking ESG criteria into account when selecting shares after 3 years generates a positive outperformance that rises continuously with a longer investment horizon. The statement is based on an analysis of 180 US companies over the period 1993 to 2010." [8]

In recent years public information regarding responsible investors has also improved considerably. Apart from the fact that numerous ESG research providers primarily focus on economic sustainability and, as Henry Schäfer has shown [9], only a small group can be called value-oriented, investors receive information on the character, quality and comparability of sustainability ratings through a study by the EÖR project group by Claudia Döpfner and Hans Albert Schneider [10].

3 What Does Sustainability Mean in the Financial Sector?

"Sustainable development means taking environmental aspects into account on an equal footing with social and economic aspects," [11] is an official definition on which political agreement could be reached because it grants equal rights to conflicting interests. The idea of the three equal pillars (in the previous quote: points of view) of sustainability "seems to be the price at which the idea of sustainability found political recognition in the 1990s," because anyone who bases sustainability policy on equal rights "of the whole (nature) with a part of the whole (society) and on top of that with a part of this part (the economy)," [12] does not want to know exactly what is important or does not want to say it so bluntly.

Sustainable business activity means the consistent conservation of substances, the preservation of the natural bases of life and production, which are intended for the totality of all life on earth (because there are no others) and thus also for future generations of mankind, i.e. must be preserved and passed on by the present generation. This shows in German the origin of the concept of "Nachhaltigkeit"/sustainability from forestry and in English the meaning of "sustain": to preserve, to supply.

The natural foundations of life [13], breathing air, preserving biodiversity and soil fertility, the abundance of fish, the climate system, raw material deposits, drinking water, etc. can only be preserved if we give them back what we have used and consumed for our purposes. If we do not give it back, we consume the inherited substance. In fact, we are parasites who have to make sure that our host, the earth on which we live, does not perish [14]. And we all know that. Unfortunately, this understanding does not always correspond to our actions. The movement set in motion by *Fridays for Future* may save us from not having to repent for our failures, but we will still be confronted with that and repent, for repentance is a limping messenger. He comes slowly but surely [15].

It is understandable that there are different opinions about what is meant by ethical-environmental and social sustainability. This also applies to ESG Research providers, which assess the sustainability performance of companies and other asset classes and the ratings often show a large divergence. The study presented by Döpfner and Schneider shows that the transparency of the research process and assessment procedures does not need to be improved as much. Although the differences here are worth mentioning, they are likely to wear off or are relatively easy to smooth out with some regulations.

In principle more problematic, is the difference in the concept of sustainability on which the ESG Research Providers base their ratings. Some are heading for a consistent ethical assessment by considering the conservation of natural and social capital as sustainable, i.e. demanding both "environmentally" and "socially" sustainable management. To this end, both the natural and the socially designed bases of life and production must be preserved in their potential, natural capital as well as social capital.

Both can only be maintained if companies do not incur losses in the longer term, so that real economic capital, the total value of private productive and human capital, is at least preserved. Economically, sustainability must be considered as we look at sustainability from environmental and social standpoints: From all three points of view, sustainability demands the preservation of environmental, social, economic and cultural substance, i.e. the preservation of the basis of life and production. This is a clear definition of sustainability based on the Brundtland Commission's definition.

Those who make sustainability progress dependent on positive financial returns have a strong motivation to postpone conservation investments. The same suspicion is (rightly) levelled at companies that attach importance to making a sustainable investment based on their individual preferences.

("Customized") valuation methods try not to be subjected to external ratings, but rather try to base everything on their own customized internal evaluations.

According to the Brundtland definition and its interpretation by the German Commission of Enquiry "Protection of Humankind and the Environment" (26.06.1998), the goal of sustainable development is that the common goods used, whether natural or socially designed, are no longer consumed, but are preserved (or restored) in their potential for future generations, in such a way that they will not be worse off in the satisfaction of their needs than those currently living. Each individual company must be measured against this goal.

This goal of an uncompromising definition of sustainability, i.e. for the preservation of substance instead of externalisation and therefore for sustainable competition, must be maintained. A sustainability rating following this definition may only award the highest rating to companies or capital investments that treat all common resources used in the same way as their own production facilities, by avoiding or compensating for any consumption of natural and social capital through appropriate replacement investments.

And the other levels of the evaluation scale must be oriented to the effect of the conservation investments: the greater the remaining externalisation, the more negative the evaluation. This would gradually ensure that renewable resources—ecosystems, the climate system, human health, social integration—can be restored and that non-renewable resources—consumed raw materials or fossil energy sources—can be reused or replaced by renewable ones within the framework of the circular economy. The ideal goal must be that no more "waste" is produced.

From a macroeconomic point of view, this must be financially viable in the long term, but the sustainability rating of the individual company must not, under any circumstances, be profit-oriented, not even additionally. This would violate the sustainability objective, which calls for more sustainable production to grow, but at the same time for less sustainable production to shrink; and it would also violate the market economy principle, which measures market performance against real sales increases and excludes all profits generated by unfair competition or pure financial manipulation.

So if we consider the dimensions of sustainable development to be not only environmental, social and cultural, but also economic, the consideration must be oriented to the real "substance" from which we live and which we must preserve. None of the three dimensions can be substituted by another, certainly not by financial capital, not even at the ECB, since those dimensions are not competing with each other, as for the return on investment, it makes no difference whether the profit is generated by maintaining or consuming the real substance.

Unfortunately, we live in Western "feel-good capitalism … in an externalisation society that functions in the mode of exploitation. Through the externalisation of constraints, one's own freedoms are created, one's own opportunities are secured through the destruction of foreign living environments, one's own circumstances are lived out through a policy at the expense of third parties." [16] PUMA and OTTO-Versand, for example, have calculated how high the externalised costs are in environmental and social terms in the context of their productions.

Sustainability in the comprehensive sense means that any externalisation of costs for the use of common resources is excluded.

4 Exclusion Criteria Versus Best-in-Class Approach

When sustainability ratings are applied, a list of exclusion criteria is often omitted. Exclusion criteria often include the following: "There is no investment in companies which manufacture weapons of war and other military equipment, which carry out animal experiments, which produce addictive substances such as alcohol and tobacco, or which violate human rights". There are some reasons why companies and capital investments should not be assessed on the basis of exclusion criteria:

The first reasons are historical. The first step in the ethical-environmental evaluation of capital investments was made through exclusion criteria. In addition, the use of exclusion criteria corresponds to an Anglo-Saxon practice and tradition. At the beginning of the 1990s, when banks in Germany were considering the ethical-environmental evaluation of capital investments, they came to the conclusion that the German-speaking and continental European markets required a more differentiated criteriology. The application with a more or less large number of exclusion criteria alone was inappropriate to our moral understanding.

For this reason, the research group Ethical-Environmental Rating presented the Frankfurt-Hohenheim Guideline in 1997, the only internationally recognized criterion to date. The guideline comprises approx. 850 individual criteria, which extend over three value dimensions, namely:

- environmental compatibility
- social compatibility
- cultural compatibility.

Together with Oekom Research AG, Munich, the project group welded this unique evaluation system into a rating concept, the Corporate Responsibility Rating (=CRR). Both in the Criteriology of the FHL and in the questionnaire of the CRR, the items are queried in a differentiated form, which are also targeted with exclusion criteria. In contrast to the examination of as many individual companies as possible according to exclusion criteria, the CRR rates as many companies as possible in a specific industry. The companies are not only evaluated individually and then excluded if necessary, but rather viewed in relation to their competitors in their own industry, i.e. they are given an ethical-environmental rating within their industry. In other words: through the Corporate Responsibility Rating an investor can select the companies that are assessed as "best-in-class".

This process not only offers a transparent opportunity to make ethical-environmental investment decisions, but also Its investment decision led by the "best-in-class system" has ethical-environmental effects on the overall economic development, because it triggers ethical competition both within the companies and between the industry sectors.

This is very helpful for an ethically oriented investor, since he not only pursues his individual interests, but at the same time sets in motion other developments in the economy that trigger ethical-environmental innovations on a broad basis and bring about a gradual change in the capital market towards more ethical performance.

The "best-in-class approach" takes into account the fundamental ethical experience that every human action has a double effect, i.e. has both positive and negative consequences. This dilemma cannot be avoided by relying on exclusion criteria. In the CRR according to the Frankfurt-Hohenheim Guidelines, no company is therefore deliberately excluded from the outset; instead, the ratings show the degree of ethical-environmental responsibility the company shows in comparison with its competitors. In addition, an opportunity and risk assessment or an analysis of the company's strengths and weaknesses makes it transparent to the companies as to how they can improve ethically. In the long term, we should continue along this path. Obviously, there are other forms which go into the same direction, i.e. engagement, measuring actual impact (i.e. through the SDGs).

However, we are becoming more and more aware that, in the medium and long term, ethical competition within and between industries will require us to expand the ethical-environmental investment spectrum as much as the climate crisis requires.

The effects that this has had and will have on the financial market are considerable, but far from sufficient for rapid and effective change in the economy if we want to mitigate or even avert a catastrophe.

To avert a catastrophe, I consider the concept of radical decarbonisation developed by Thomas Weber together with Nana Karlstetter and Gerhard Hofmann to be effective. If we want to make the continued existence of mankind and the world possible, we must become aware of the approaching climatic catastrophe so as to transform our behaviour to drastically reduce world-wide CO^2 emissions. How is this possible?

The concept "starts with the reduction of the release of previously fossil-bound CO^2, because the environmental necessity demands an absolute quantitative upper limit and thus an almost complete cessation of this release in the future as a prerequisite for all further transformation steps …." [17] On the basis of the current CO^2 release and an upper limit for global warming of 1.5 degrees Celsius, the global CO^2 budget available within the upper limit should be largely exhausted in 20 years at the latest—even with a drastic continuous reduction. The proposal therefore aims at implementation (decarbonisation) in 20 years.

The aim of the proposal is to shape the transformation socially in such a way that it meets the equality requirement necessary for the acceptance of the transformation by providing all citizens with an equal CO^2 budget—i.e. an equal share of natural resources—and by ensuring that the transformation does not result in only the rich being able to consume CO^2, i.e. that financial resources are redistributed from "wrong" to "right" consumption. In this context, "right" means avoiding products and services that release CO^2. This requires that citizens, as consumers, be given an incentive and the opportunity to receive an income that they would not have without this transformation, i.e. that a prerequisite be created for the acceptance of the necessary transformation.

The working concepts of “transformation capacity”, “transformation income” (sometimes called a carbon dividend), etc. are to be understood as transitional concepts (“transition concepts”). They can certainly be understood as preliminary stages for a “natural asset” to be determined after the phase of transition, from which a “basic natural income” is financed.

The proposal starts with CO^2 emissions, for which the transformation provides for an almost complete decarbonisation of economic life. In this respect, the concrete proposal can also be described as a “decarbonisation capacity”/“decarbonisation income”. A future basic natural income will then be based on the total natural resource use or material flows [18]. This will generate part of the capital required for the transformation of society. According to the United Nations Conference on Trade and Development (UNCTAD), between USD 3.3 and 4.5 trillion annually in public, private, national and international funds are needed to cover the financial requirements for the major transformation and implementation of Agenda 2030 for sustainable development with its 17 Sustainable Development Goals (SDGs)—and only in developing countries. This is also a challenge for the ECB [19].

5 ECB and Sustainability

As Harald Bolsinger made clear in his petition to the European Commission, “the European Central Bank (ECB) is indirectly involved in undermining the fundamental values of the European Union. This is done on a daily basis by trading in securities linked to breaches of the Charter of Fundamental Rights of the European Union. The impact of this action may have a significant impact on the further development of the European Union, given the large volumes of transactions carried out by the ECB.” [20]

5.1 What Are the Causes?

One cause—perhaps even the origin—is the stimulation of growth and financial assets by the German Act to Promote Economic Growth and Financial Assets (StabG) of 1967. The act came into being under the chancellorship of Kiesinger and Economics Minister Schiller. In the interest of a more or less even economic growth, the ideas of John Maynard Keynes came into play and replaced the previously predominant ordoliberal thinking. During my economics studies in Munich 1963—1965 I remember the lectures of Prof. Pfister e.g. on “General Economics and Economic Policy”. Nature, labour and capital were taught to us as the basis or means of production of the economy as equivalent and equally to be considered means of economic development. Or to put it another way: natural capital as the totality of the natural goods of production and social capital as the totality of the production prerequisites provided by the respective culture.

The StabG was accompanied by a prioritisation and absolute setting of financial capital with the result that natural capital and social capital could be instrumentalised for the externalisation of costs in favour of financial capital. The result is impure capitalism, i.e. the consumption of natural capital, as the climate crisis clearly shows us. Social capital is also being consumed. Income disparities are widening globally, the number of unused workers is increasing, monotonous shopping streets are emerging, and so on. This is not a sustainable economic development, neither from an economic point of view nor even less from an environmental and social perspective.

This development was reinforced by the consequences of the German Agenda 2010. Unfortunately, the critical objections to the StabG, e.g. by the Enquete Commission "Growth, Prosperity, Quality of Life" (2010–2013) or in 1990 by members of Bündnis 90/die Grünen in the German Bundestag, were not successful.

In my opinion, another reason lies in the person of Mario Draghi, the outgoing ECB President. On the one hand, he is praised as an outstanding thinker and financial specialist. Peer Steinbrück says of him: "In a major crisis, he represented the only institution in Europe capable of taking action with the ECB and was condemned to be a substitute actor in politics." [21] But he does ask us to consider whether, given the current high level of liquidity, the "negative interest rate phase" must be abandoned. Steinbrück is not alone in this opinion. "Zero interest rates and bond purchases have consequences for the distribution of wealth in society" [22] and—as I see it—consequences for the preservation of natural capital and the climate crisis. Jens Weidmann, President of the Bundesbank, also opposed "Draghi's policy of easy money .... the consequences of the recent further reduction in the key interest rate are so clearly felt in the lives of many citizens that even former supporters find that things should not go on like this. In an open letter, former central bankers from Germany, France, Austria and the Netherlands have opposed the ECB's previous monetary policy [23]. Draghi is considered a respected specialist. But he also gives the impression that he did not sufficiently discuss his considerations and decisions in discourse with other experts and their perspectives. He seems to be a lonely decision-maker. That is dangerous, because: we may live on specialists, but we should avoid dying from their monologues.

References

1. Jean Ziegler, in: Tahir Chaudhry, Süddeutsche Zeitung, 2./3.9.2017, Nr. 202, Seite 50. See: Jean Ziegler. Der schmale Grat der Hoffnung. Meine gewonnenen und verlorenen Kämpfe und die, die wir gemeinsam gewinnen werden, München 2017.
2. Webster, Peter, Ethical Investment Research Service, London; in: Roche, Peter/Hoffmann, Johannes/Homolka, Walter, Hg., Ethische Geldanlagen. Kapital auf neuen Wegen, Frankfurt 1992, p. 62-77.
3. Hoffmann, J. /Ott, K. /Scherhorn, G., Hg. , Ethische Kriterien für die Bewertung von Unternehmen – Frankfurt-Hohenheimer Leitfaden, Frankfurt/Stuttgart 1997
4. Information: www.cric-online.org

5. Information: www.forum-ng.org; see also the very informative last newsletter Nr. 95, August 2019.
6. http://www.gsi-alliance.org/wp-content/uploads/2019/06/GSIR_Review2018F.pdf
7. Information: jdd@united-sustainability.com
8. Zitiert nach oekom, Corporate Responsibility Review 2012, p. 14.
9. Schäfer, H.; Hauser-Dietz, A.; Preller, E.S., Transparenzstudie zur Beschreibung ausgewählter international verbreiteter Rating-Systeme zur Erfassung von Corporate Social Responsibility, Gütersloh/Stuttgart 2004
10. Döpfner, C.; Schneider, H.A.; Nachhaltigkeitsratings auf dem Prüfstand. Pilotstudie zu Charakter, Qualität und Vergleichbarkeit von Nachhaltigkeitsratings, Erkelenz 2012, see: https://www.cric-online.org/images/individual_upload/publikationen/nachhaltigkeitsstudie2012.pdf.
11. Rat für Nachhaltige Entwicklung, see *www.nachhaltigkeitsrat.de/nachhaltigkeit*.
12. Meyer-Abich, Klaus Michael (2001): Nachhaltigkeit – ein kulturelles, bisher aber chancenloses Wirtschaftsziel, in: Zeitschrift für Wirtschafts- und Unternehmensethik 2 (3), 303f.
13. see Art. 20a Grundgesetz: „Der Staat schützt auch die natürlichen Lebensgrundlagen."
14. See Kaltenbrunner, Gerd-Klaus, Schmarotzer breiten sich aus. Parasitismus als Lebensform. Die öffentlichen Verschwender/Zur Philosophie des Parasitären/Der Staat und das ‚Soziale'/ Paradoxien des unbeschwerten Menschseins ... München 1981.
15. See for the acceptance of repentance in other contexts: Käppner, Joachim, Die späte Reue der Konzerne, in Süddeutsche Zeitung 28./29.Mai 2014, Nr. 122, Seite 17.
16. St. Lessenich, Neben uns die Sintflut. Westlicher Wohlfühlkapitalismus lebt nicht über seine Verhältnisse. Er lebt über die Verhältnisse anderer, in: Süddeutsche Zeitung, 30.10.2014, Nr. 250, 9.
17. Weber, Thomas, Politischer Vorschlag zu einem „Transformationsvermögen"/ „Transformationseinkommen"als Gestaltungs- und Steuerungsinstrument in der unausweichlichen sozial-ökologischen Transformation. Cited from manuscript in preperation (21.2.2019), und https://www.agentur-zukunft.eu/2019/06/111-vollstaendige-dekarbonisierung-budgetorientiert/
18. Hofmann, Gerhard/Karlstetter, Nana/Weber, Thomas, , Politischer Vorschlag zu einem „Transformationsvermögen"/ „Transformationseinkommen"als Gestaltungs- und Steuerungsinstrument in der unausweichlichen sozial-ökologischen Transformation. Manuskript from 21.2.2019, cited from Hoffmann, Johannes, Meine Träume zu Kirchfinanzen und Kirchenentwicklung in Deutschland, Genf 2019, p. 79ff.
19. Zitiert nach: Stremlau, Silke, Nachhaltigkeit als Chance – Haltung, Regulatorik und Querdenken im Finanzmarkt, manuscript, p. 3.
20. Bolsinger, Harald, Petition from May 2017; http://www.wirtschaftsethik.biz/publikationen/verpflichtung-der-Europäischen-Zentralbank-auf-EU-Grundrechte
21. Gammelin, Cerstin, Interview, Die Geldpolitik hat ihre Handlungsfähigkeit verloren. Maria Draghi, der scheidende Präsident der Europäischen Zentralbank, hat vieles richtig gemacht, findet Peer Steinbrück – etwa mit Niedrigzinsen geholfen, als die Euro-Staaten Reformen versäumten. Dann aber habe er den entscheidenden Moment verpasst, in: Süddeutsche Zeitung, 22.10.2019, Nr. 244, p. 22.
22. Zydra, Markus, Neue Frankfurter Schule. Schluß mit Notenbanker-Fachsprech? Was die designierte EZB-Chefin Lagarde anders machen will als ihre Vorgänger, in: Süddeutsche Zetung, 3.9.2019, Nr. 203, p. 17
23. Gammelin, Cerstin, Jens Weidmann. Geldpolitischer Oppositionschef in der EZB, in: Süddeutsche Zeitung, 17.10.2019, Nr.240, p. 4

Ethical Standards Beyond Monetary Policy: Approaches to a Philosophical Foundation

Bernd Villhauer

Abstract This paper illustrates why the European Central Bank has obligations that go far beyond economic and financial market-related responsibilities. As a European institution, it is committed to a core set of values, especially with regard to the preservation of human rights. These obligations are part of its contribution to the creation of a social and ecological market economy in Europe and do not conflict with its regulatory and market-related responsibilities.

The tasks of the European Central Bank (ECB) and the matters it deals with are wide-ranging. The 1992 Maastricht Treaty and the 2007 Lisbon Treaty defined the fundamental elements of what the ECB is and how it should function. Since the Lisbon Treaty, the ECB has been defined as an inherent institution of the EU: like the European Parliament, the European Council, the Council of the European Union, the European Commission, the Court of Justice of the European Union and the European Court of Auditors.

What is the specific responsibility and jurisdiction of the ECB as an EU institution as well as a European institution? It is important to bear this in mind at a fundamental level, for Europe is not only a community of peace and economic togetherness, but also a community of shared-values based on philosophical and ethical principles. These values also bind us together as Europeans, and these same values will allow us to create a sustainable future.

B. Villhauer (✉)
Weltethos-Institut at the University of Tübingen, Tübingen, Germany
e-mail: villhauer@weltethos-institut.org

H. Bolsinger et al. (eds.), *The European Central Bank as a Sustainability Role Model*, Sustainable Finance, https://doi.org/10.1007/978-3-030-55450-7_2

1 Europe as a Community of Shared Values

The question now is: how can we actually turn our pretty soap-box speeches into a concrete reality? In order to answer this question, the European contracts and treaties must be examined closely. The European founding documents reveal a threefold origin in terminology as well as in objectives:

- From the philosophical heritage of ancient Greece and Rome
- From the Christian set of values and its perception of humankind
- From the eighteenth century Enlightenment.

These elements have contributed to a European understanding of values as a basis for national and transnational structures; the dynamics of the European unification process with all its paradoxes and contradictions will be better understood if we recognize this variety and hold ourselves back from pitting one element against the other. The shared-values as a whole give the European project its specific identity.

In order to gain a better understanding of the intellectual foundations of Europe, the major speeches and announcements of important actors must be taken into account. It is imperative to know how Robert Schuman, Konrad Adenauer, Alcide de Gasperi, Walter Hallstein, Jacques Delors, Helmut Kohl and Jean-Claude Juncker described the European shared-value system. We will then have a better understanding of the hopes and goals with which our European "home" was built.

This has been put into concrete terms in European treaties such as the Maastricht Treaty, which merges the previous unification treaties into the various European Communities (EEC, ECSC, EURATOM). However, the concrete formulations in the founding documents of the EU must always be understood within the framework of their philosophical and ethical prerequisites. These lead to a specifically European conception of humankind which can be expanded into individual values.

A series[1] edited by Clemens Sedmak lists: Solidarity, Freedom, Equality, Tolerance, Peace and Human Dignity. However in 2010 and 2018 the European Commission conducted a survey to gain insight into what Europeans believed to be inherent "European values" and obtained the following results: peace, human rights, democracy, rule of law, solidarity/support of others, respect for human life, freedom of the individual, respect for other cultures, equality, tolerance, self-realization and religion. Interestingly, there was a noticeable shift of emphasis on certain values from November 2010 to March 2018. In 2018 "peace" was at the top of the list with 39%, in 2010 "human rights" and "democracy" were both at the top with 38% each. The proportion of people who found "none of these values" important was 3% (2010) and 5% (2018).[2]

---

[1] Clemens Sedmak (ed.), Grundwerte Europas, Darmstadt (WBG), 7 volumes, 2010-2017

[2] Europäische Kommission: Eurobarometer 89: Die europäische Bürgerschaft, 03/2018, Eurobarometer 74: Die öffentliche Meinung in der Europäischen Union, 11/2010

The Treaty on European Union, Article 2 reads as follows: "The values on which the Union is founded are respect for human dignity, freedom, democracy, equality, the rule of law and respect for human rights, including the rights of persons belonging to minorities. These values are common to the Member States in a society in which pluralism, non-discrimination, tolerance, justice, solidarity and equality between women and men prevail." Such statements cannot be properly interpreted unless it is clear that they are intended to build a framework of action based on ethical convictions and standards. This also applies to economic activities within Europe, as well as to our foreign trade relations.

Article 3, paragraph 3 states, "The Union shall establish an internal market. It shall work for the sustainable development of Europe based on balanced economic growth and price stability, a highly competitive social market economy, aiming at full employment and social progress, and a high level of protection and improvement of the quality of the environment … " According to the EU, then, it is a social and ecological market economy. It is prepared to combine economic development with social and political objectives instead of pitting them against each other. This was made clear as early as May 9th 1950 in the famous Schuman Declaration, "The French Government proposes that Franco-German production of coal and steel as a whole be placed under a common high authority, within the framework of an organization open to the participation of the other countries of Europe. the pooling of coal and steel production should immediately provide for the setting up of common foundations for economic development as a first step in the federation of Europe, and will change the destinies of those regions which have long been devoted to the manufacture of munitions of war, of which they have been the most constant victims."

The Treaty of Lisbon states that the EU should develop into a "competitive social market economy." Ensuring prosperity and full employment should go hand in hand with preserving employers' rights. It is no coincidence then that the treaty also declares the EU's accession to the European Convention on Human Rights.

It begs the question then, how can we connect the economy and the shared-values in the context of the European institutions? How can traditions become guidelines for action and what does this mean for the ECB?

2 Values and Law

One of the classic mechanisms of arbitration and implementation is the law. The implementation of ethical principles via legal means must be required and promoted. European law can certainly be understood as an implementing body of a shared understanding of values, also with regard to the ECB's policy. The European Community sees itself as a constitutional entity. Its actions and the role of the institutions are laid down in treaties. All treaties, from the Treaty of Rome (1957) to the Treaty of Lisbon (2007), were repeatedly amended, construed in debates and reshaped in detail. The European Central Bank, with its legal foundation, is also the subject of such discussions, with both the various national concerns and the EU's position in world markets dictating contexts for discussion.

But this is where the fundamental issue of the ECB's independence comes into play. The central bank was designed as an independent body with an extensive scope for action for good reason, and it has been assigned the main task of ensuring price stability for equally good reason. How can its mandate be understood in this context? Clearly, the ECB must be independent of political influence in its decision making. It was not created to support the economic policies of individual actors; it must make decisions for the good of the European community as a whole and maintain a long term perspective. It can only do both as an independent institution.

However, it is also inherently embedded in fundamental European norms such as the recognition of human rights, and therefore also dependent on these norms. These shared values can be understood as essential elements and prerequisites of the ordoliberal framework which the ECB, like all other EU institutions, must adhere to. The ECB is free to act independently within this framework. The drafting of the ECB's price stability policy also occurred independently within this framework.

3 The Law as the Only Available Implementation Measure Within the Context of a Social and Ecological Market Economy?

Is this legal dimension sufficient? The connection between law and values can be addressed with this question: where does the relation with codified law begin, and where does it end? When must law be complemented by ethical reflection in theory and an ethos in practice? The age-old debate on "law" vs. "justice," i.e. on the normative aspects of law, cannot be addressed here. We leave this to Feuerbach, Radbruch, Geiger, Kelsen, Fikentscher and Rüthers, all of whom can give insight into this complex question. The former President of the Constitutional Court of Baden-Württemberg, Eberhard Stilz, described the relationship between law and ethics as follows, "… the totality of moral norms, i.e. the ethos, is an indispensable foundation and reference for legal norms."[3]

He argues that the supreme law within our legal system is also our most fundamental value: the inviolability of human dignity. To further illustrate his point he quotes the so-called Böckenförde Dilemma, which I will cite here in shortened form, "the liberal, secularized state lives by requirements that it cannot guarantee itself (…) On the one hand the liberal state can only survive if the freedom it grants its citizens is regulated from within by the moral substance of each individual and the homogeneity of society itself. On the other hand, it cannot guarantee these internal regulatory forces on its own, by means of legal coercion and authoritative decrees, without relinquishing its liberal character, and, on a secularized level slip

[3] In: Ulrich Hemel (ed.), Weltethos für das 21. Jahrhundert, Freiburg i.Br. 2019, pg. 140

back into totalitarianism from which it once led society out of in the Confessional Wars."[4]

I believe it to be of use to relate this insight, which initially refers to religious traditions and norms, to the sphere of the European legal system. First of all, it is important to note that the European system is very different from what the above citation deems the "state." Next we must ask whether or not, and if so how, the concept of "homogeneity" plays a role. If homogeneity is not defined too narrowly, as cultural, linguistic or even ethnic homogeneity, then we can broaden our view of living together on the basis of shared-values, a European understanding of what it means to be humans, a European understanding of the world and also of the law. This is not only theoretical in nature, but based on experience; anyone who has traveled outside of Europe, whether it be to Ghana or Paraguay, to China or Korea, or even to the USA or Russia, has surely noticed how specifically European her or she is, and undoubtedly realized what connects him or her with a Portuguese, a Polish, or a Dutch person.

It is interesting that Böckenförde explicitly refers to the establishment of peace after the series of religious wars, which were inherently European conflicts. He also addresses another aspect that is important to fully comprehend the moral foundations or parameters of legal provisions: the interpretation of legal norms, as well as their implementation and practical application in everyday life. In a liberal or free society, a person must constantly make the conscious choice to comply with legal norms. They must also interpret them in a way that corresponds to the overall context and objectives of the legal system. Their individual ethos and their ethical competence to speak and act in the right way must complement the legal guidelines; in essence breathe life into them. "Compliance" must be complemented by "conscience"—a constant check of one's conduct and one's conscience.

This applies to both the individual as well as the collective level. The economic and financial policy of the EU must also be subject to a constant process of critical self-reflection. This critical reflection has two advantages: on the one hand, it enables internal learning processes both in the specific field of financial policy and in the larger field of European unification. On the other hand, it abets international legitimacy, strengthens unity and imparts vitality. This is more important than ever in view of the current rise of national populisms and the crisis of multilateral organizations and agreements.[5]

---

[4] Quote from: Hemel 2019, pg. 143

[5] A reference concerning the threat to the regulatory and arbitrational role of the World Trade Organization (WTO) in the current (December 2019) world situation must be included here.

4 The ECB's Contribution to a European Social and Ecological Market Economy

Alongside a variety of measures, the ECB practices enormous interventions with its purchasing programs. Broad, sweeping statements ("whatever it takes..!") regarding future policies inherently impact and change the situation of all market participants. This power must go hand in hand with responsibility and accountability. Ethical competences must be a vital requirement in the political and economic sphere as well. The social market economy in Germany is a perfect example of how an ethical framework does not destroy the market, but shapes it instead. Looking at the German economy, ethics is clearly not a limiting factor, but rather a driver of innovation. Therefore the "responsible finance approach" also opens doors, not to restrict the financial market, but to transform it.

Pricing mechanisms play a special role here. It is worth recalling the discussions regarding the Corporate Sector Purchase Programme (CSPP) and the criticism of economists as to whether the wrong incentives for price formation were given, whether misallocations were abetted and whether there was a risk of market distortion. It is not easy to find a balance, but much like the adherence to the standards of fundamental human rights and social norms, we must find a way to design a sustainable market that does justice to the current situation and paves the way for a social and ecological market economy. To this end, however, the naive idea of self-regulating markets must be put into question. Theorists can learn a lot from practitioners who have long been confronted with political markets or pricing mechanisms in which externalizations of the costs of environmental destruction are not factored into the price.

5 Market Conforming and Non-market Based Policies

Of particular interest to researchers are the specific characteristics of the financial markets that allow for modelling. It must be noted that it is not the purpose of this paper to delve into detail regarding the markets types which are suitable for shaping within the framework of the social market economy. It is obvious, however, that in particular the financial markets, with their political dependencies, their powerful stakeholders, their monopolies and oligopolies and their mixture of a high degree of regulation regarding certain national concerns and uncontrolled growth on a global level, definitely do not correspond to the market-ideal found in textbooks.

The interaction between the law and compliance complicated by the many gray zones renders voluntary legal compliance insufficient; instead the EU institutions must constantly question whether they are acting on the basis of the shared-values. A region like Europe, which is becoming increasingly unimportant in military and economic terms, is particularly dependent on moral authority.

This is not necessarily connected to a singular "European identity" or with encroaching bureaucratic standardizations. It is precisely this unity in diversity, this awareness of common goals and obligations, e.g. the protection of human rights that can offer Europe a way out of its present crises.

The realization that economic dynamism must also be utilized in order to ensure a successful coexistence lies at the heart of the matter. Nothing can effectively put a stop to today's market forces—but it is possible and crucial to control the direction and dosage of these forces, as well as the creation and modelling of specific market situations. Within this context it is helpful to analyze the determining factors regarding a European market economy which fosters people and the environment through the lens of institutional economics.

6 Future Tasks for the President: Christine Lagarde's Decisions

What will be the development of the ECB's concrete policy in the near future? This depends on many factors, such as the global economic environment and nationalist and populist movements in the various countries. However, the policy of the new ECB President Lagarde will also play a major role in this development. There are many indications, based on what has been made public regarding Christine Lagarde's plans, that sustainability will play a greater role, at least the tendency seems to be there. Two major recurring themes in her speeches are "responsible finance" and "sustainable finance." Will she really put more emphasis on a more sustainable Europe? In the past, she has repeatedly taken a stand for a more sustainable and ethically minded financial system.

Any actions taken in the direction of accountability and sustainability will not only presumably harmonize with the "Green New Deal" announced by Ursula von der Leyen, President of the European Commission, but also mutually reinforce one another. However, resistance from the ECB's Executive Board, and/or from the central banks of member states is also to be expected. A well- known voice of opposition is the president of the Bundesbank, Jens Weidtmann, who stated at an ECB event in Frankfurt in October 2019, "I believe that a resolute and effective climate policy is necessary—but only by implementing the right measures and via democratically legitimized actors." He continues, clearly taking an opposing stance in light of demands for the purchase of "green" bonds and the creation of a sustainable portfolio: What measures should be taken, what behavior should be encouraged or punished? These are political questions that elected governments and parliaments must answer."[6]

It is within Christina Lagarde's power to put this in a new perspective. At the hearing before ECON, the European Parliament's Committee on Economic and

[6] Quotes from: „Handelsblatt", 29.10.2019

Monetary Affairs, which was part of her nomination process, she stated, "… the discussion on whether, and if so how central banks and banking supervisors can contribute to mitigating climate change is at an early stage but should be seen as a priority." However, she also pointed out the leadership responsibility of the European Commission, "The most appropriate, first-best policy response and initiatives primarily fall outside the realm of central bank policies."[7] It remains to be seen what this will mean for the ECB.

Bibliography

1. Markus Brunnermeier, Harold James, Jean-Pierre Landau, Euro. Der Kampf der Wirtschaftskulturen, München (C.H. Beck) 2018
2. Europa-Recht (dtv Beck Texte), München (C.H. Beck) 2017[27]
3. Nils Goldschmidt/Michael Wohlgemuth (ed.) Grundtexte zur Freiburger Tradition der Ordnungsökonomik, Tübingen (Mohr Siebeck) 2008
4. Michael Heine/Hansjörg Herr, Die Europäische Zentralbank. Eine kritische Einführung in die Strategie und Politik der EZB und die Probleme in der EWU, Marburg (Metropolis) 2008[3]
5. Ulrich Hemel (ed.), Weltethos für das 21. Jahrhundert, Freiburg i.Br. (Herder) 2019
6. Hans Joas/Klaus Wiegandt (ed.), Die kulturellen Werte Europas, Frankfurt a.M. (Fischer) 2010[5]
7. Clemens Sedmak (ed.), Grundwerte Europas, Darmstadt (WBG), 7 volumes, 2010-2017
8. Alexander Thiele, Die Europäische Zentralbank: Von technokratischer Behörde zu politischem Akteur?, Tübingen (Mohr Siebeck) 2019

[7] Quotes from: „The Parliament", 06.09.2019

Fundamental Rights in the Core Business of the ECB: No Issue?!

Experience with the EU Petition 429/2017

Harald J. Bolsinger

Abstract Petition 0429/2017 has been brought forward by Prof. Harald Bolsinger. In this article he describes backgrounds and developments around the petition. The petition, submitted on May the 8th 2017, addressed the investments policy of the ECB. Compliance with EU Fundamental Rights, it claimed, should be specifically included into the eligibility for EU owned assets. As Bolsinger explains, at the moment the ECB is involved in violations of the Charter of Fundamental Rights of the European Union through possession and trading of unethical securities.

1 How It All Began

Our world is facing major economic, ecological, cultural and social challenges, which all influential players must help to overcome—including the financial industry. This experience report explains the origins of the EU petition 0429/2017 and its development until the end of 2019. This paper describes the process from the petitioner's subjective point of view and thus conveys his personal perception and opinion.

1.1 Climate Challenge and Beyond

The earth's temperature will most likely increase by nearly 5 degrees Celsius by 2050 if all companies worldwide were to follow the production of the companies in the DAX 30! The global warming contribution of the DAX 30 companies ranges from just under 1 to up to 11 degrees Celsius. This would surely result in the utter ruin of the earth and humanity as a whole would be threatened. This climate indicator

H. J. Bolsinger (✉)
Faculty for Economics and Business Administration, University of Applied Sciences Würzburg-Schweinfurt (FHWS), Münzstraße 12, Würzburg, Germany
e-mail: bolsinger@orientationcompetence.info

H. Bolsinger et al. (eds.), *The European Central Bank as a Sustainability Role Model*, Sustainable Finance, https://doi.org/10.1007/978-3-030-55450-7_3

is known as "X-Degree-Compatibility" (XDC) and expresses, on the basis of scientific data, by what degree the earth would warm up by 2050 if the behavior of the company in question were to be adopted by all companies worldwide. (see www.right-basedonscience.de/en) Similar estimations can be made regarding all other global challenges focusing on a sustainable global society. The results are equally frightening and have opened our eyes to the fact that "business as usual" is no longer compatible with the goal of a dignified and secure future. Many of our current supply chains and production methods are still fraught with human rights violations, environmental degradation and corruption, even though we operate within a global regulatory framework designed to counter act such unacceptable and contemptible behavior. The various analyses of established sustainability rating organizations prove that the number of ethical issues in companies has increased in all industries (see e.g. data from www.issgovernance.com/esg/)

Profitable business models that have implemented unethical and destructive management almost as a matter of course can only be changed holistically by depriving them of the economic basis for their ethically questionable behavior. Not only can consumers exert influence by voluntarily changing their consumer behavior, but financial market players can also indirectly influence ethical economic activity instead of sharing responsibility for unethical economic behavior. Commercial banks and insurance companies can make a positive contribution with their investment policy, as can central banks. For Europe, "can" does not apply to the Central Bank, instead it is a "must" that has already been codified in terms of regulatory policy, as Bernd Vilhauer's previous contribution makes clear.

1.2 Hidden Places of Horror

While accompanying a courageous, small universal bank in Germany on its way from a regular bank to a bank focusing on sustainability, I noticed some important points in the reorganization of the investment policy which affect all banks equally; it is within the decision-making authority and responsibility of the bank itself to invest its funds in areas that have either beneficial or detrimental impacts on society. Due to the widely prevailing view that investment decisions are not ethical decisions, but rather a balancing act between return, risk and liquidity, horrible investment decisions regarding treasury and investment policy are not unusual. Commercial banks invest in a wide range of companies that quite obviously destroy the environment; they invest in large banks that have already been convicted in the past for their corrupt and criminal behavior, or even in companies that exploit people treating them like slaves. How can this happen? First of all the blindness of the decision-makers regarding the ethical dimension of their investment decisions is to blame. However this can easily change if we take the blinders off by creating a clear definition of exclusionary ethical criteria and a sustainability rating prior to the investment decision. Whether you're a bank teller at a small bank or the CEO of a billion-dollar institution, it's clear to everyone that a willingness to invest signals the belief that the business in question shall grow or at least remain as profitable as it is at the time of investment. Nobody invests with the intention that his investment will be lost or that the return expectations will not be met. Investment and lending therefore have a clear normative dimension: what the money is invested in is regarded as desirable, worthy of promotion and ethically good. With his money, the investor enables growth and continuity of the business in which he invests. However, countless commercial banks act as if this is not the case. They publicly present themselves as trustworthy, honest and credible having no intention to do anyone or anything harm. Unfortunately, their investment activities reflect exactly the opposite. They often green wash their actions by putting solar panels on the roof, offering Fair Trade coffee to their customers and printing on recycled paper. At the same time, however, billions are invested in coal-fired power plants, exploitative business models and large banks that actively promote tax avoidance and conduct wealth management for war criminals. These depots or "places of horror" are hidden from the public and remain undisclosed for reasons of competition policy.

1.3 The ECB as Role Model

While commercial banks can largely determine their own exclusion criteria for investments, this has never been the case for the European Central Bank. The minimum requirement regarding the ethics of this European institution's portfolio policy is laid down in a binding agreement in the Charter of Fundamental Rights of the European Union. The Lisbon Treaties empower the EU Charter of Fundamental Rights as the primary law in all European institutions. This is also true for the ECB! All the activities of the ECB as an European institution must, therefore, comply with the codified values of the Charter of Fundamental Rights. This is the sober regulatory framework that is already in place and this is how the ordoliberal principle of our European eco-social market economy functions. This is also the reason why in theory the ECB is a role model for the commercial banks to not participate in and not promote environmental destruction, the acceptance of child labor as well as slave labor, the facilitation of corruption and fraud in its financial market policy, which is designed independently of day-to-day political influence. Upon first glance I thought monetary policy does not need to go hand in hand with companies that commit the above-mentioned crimes in order to function. However, on closer inspection, I discovered that the ECB does not care at all about its exclusionary criteria or has even been remotely held accountable to them by anyone so far! It became clear to me why so many, and I mean *so many,* commercial banks do not waste a single thought on the indirect impact of their investments. For the great regulator, the ECB, does not do it either—although it has been obliged to do so for more than a decade. So why should the small commercial banks be obligated to do so?

The reason for this blatant ignorance is quite simple and wearisome—it is to maintain a so called "market neutrality." Participation in corrupt business and targeted environmental destruction is owed to market neutrality—that's the way the world works, that's the way the financial market works, and anyone who questions this clearly has no idea how the highly complex monetary policy processes work?! However, when this ridiculous belief is questioned, another argument rears its head to block the simple demand for the Central Bank to conform to the Charter of Fundamental rights: the independence of the ECB. The Treaty on the Functioning of the European Union, clearly defined the Central Bank's independence strictly forbidding the exertion of so-called political influence. This seems to include demanding respecting the fundamental rights. It does not take an expert to notice immediately that this is completely illogical and cannot be true. Monetary freedom does not undermine the regulatory boundaries of Europe's Central Bank. The independence of the ECB is not a license to disregard fundamental rights. This is also not written anywhere in the Treaty on the Functioning of the European Union! Otherwise, the ECB would be an institution that is unassailable and without accountability to the courts having unlimited power, not beholden to even the most basic values and standards.

As an institution of the European Union, the ECB holds an unparalleled role among the central banks. The European Commission shapes the ECB's regulatory policy in the form of guidelines and the ECB is accountable to the European Parliament as the supervisory body and guardian of fundamental rights. It is therefore a matter of course that the ECB, in its financing practices, preserves and respects European values in the form of fundamental rights, or at least does not violate the values of the European Charter of Fundamental Rights in its business dealings. On the road to a sustainable European financial system, respect for fundamental rights in the ECB's business conduct is at the very beginning of all initiatives. If the ECB acts as a role model within the framework of the Charter of Fundamental Rights, which is binding, this will have an impact on all financial market players. If the ECB does not, all other political initiatives for a more sustainable financial system will be completely useless!

1.4 Ethical Blindness in the Eurosystem

Throughout the entire Eurosystem, financial technocratic criteria are considered at an incredible level of complexity, checked daily, reported by all commercial banks and severely sanctioned by regulators and the ECB. But the ethical quality of investments and portfolios is almost completely ignored in the day-to-day business of the Central Bank itself, except for individual issues such as money laundering and international sanctions! The eligibility criteria for securities and assets for monetary policy operations with the ECB do not explicitly specify restrictions of any ethical nature. The terms "sustainability," "human rights" and "fundamental rights" do not appear at all in the relevant guidelines. The guidelines and regulations are ethically completely blind! Sustainability ratings for the assessment of the quality of securities, banks and other financial market players are therefore simply not carried out by the Central Bank, nor are they reduced to the criteria laid down in the Charter of

Fundamental Rights. The ECB does not follow through on its obligation to counter or avoid infringements of fundamental rights. This is an intolerable and scandalous breach of due diligence, as data for such audits are publicly available in the market. They could be used at any time by the Central Bank to conduct systematic checks of compliance with the fundamental rights. This was the reason to examine, for the first time, the securities accepted by the ECB as collateral for loans regarding ethical controversies. The results showed that around one fifth of the securities are linked to numerous ethical controversies which do not comply with the EU Charter of Fundamental Rights as a minimum standard. These considerations led to the decision to submit a petition to the European Parliament in 2017.

2 The EU Petition 429/2017

The original petition was submitted on May 8th, 2017 in German and can be found in Annex A.1.

2.1 Content Overview

The simple problem: the ECBs core business does not take the EU Fundamental Rights into account! All banks of the Eurozone must obtain credit from the ECB. The ECB provides such credit against collateral. The volume of the "eligible marketable assets" for use as collateral is 15,199 billion € in the second quarter of 2020. This means it has an incredibly large influence on the EU single market and the EU citizens. The ECB's eligibility criteria for collateral and other assets does not include compliance with the European Charter of Fundamental Rights, so there is a total ethical blindness in the financial market regarding inherent EU values. ESG-controversy scans (=common sustainability ratings for controversies in ecology, social and governance topics) prove that 20% of the ECBs "eligible marketable assets" are involved in severe ethical controversies! (see www.wirtschaftsethik.biz/centralbank) Therefore the ECB is a part of the infamous club of financing institutions that are ignoring and defecting on fundamental rights and thereby supporting and fostering unethical business practices within the EU.

The solution is also very simple; Compliance with EU Fundamental Rights must be specifically included into the eligibility criteria for ECB owned assets. As an EU institution the ECB must respect the fundamental rights in its business conduct. Article 6 (1) TEU shows the unconditional legally binding nature of the Charter and Articles 51 and 52 of the Charter clearly state that it is without conditions legally binding for the ECB. The TFEU does grant an incredible amount of independence to the ECB, but not independence of the EU Charter of Fundamental rights! Respecting fundamental rights is a regulatory MUST for all EU institutions and fundamental rights are the limits of all actions, also for the ECB's actions.

The website of the EU-Petition committee has summarized the petition in its own words: “The petitioner calls upon the European Parliament to state its position on the ‚indirect violations’ of the EU Charter of Fundamental Rights by the European Central Bank (ECB). The petitioner is of the view that the ECB, an important EU institution, should change the manner of operationalizing its minimum reserve requirements for credit institutions. Namely, the petitioner calls for a change to the manner in which the operational framework of the ECB is currently regulated. The purpose of changing the regulatory framework would be (1) to secure compliance with ethical standards and fundamental rights by ECB-approved issuers of securities and (2) to link compliance with the minimum reserve requirements with an independent, publicly available sustainability ratings agency. To support his petition, the petitioner provides an analysis of data made available by Oekom Research AG, a global rating agency active in the area of sustainable investment. According to the petitioner, the analysis shows that up to 88% of companies whose securities are currently traded within the context of the ECB-approved minimum reserve requirements program do not comply with multiple provisions of the EU Charter of Fundamental Rights. The companies listed include Airbus Group, Eni SpA, Wells Fargo & Co., Anheuser-Busch InBev SA/NV and Lafarge Holcim Ltd. The alleged Charter violations include business malpractices in the areas of environmental degradation, child labor, worker exploitation, and trade in arms.” (https://www.europarl.europa.eu/petitions/en/petition/content/0429%252F2017/html/Petition-No-0429%252F2017-by-Harald-Bolsinger-%2528German%2529-on-the-compliance-of-the-European-Central-Bank-with-the-EU-Charter-of-Fundamental-Rights)

This summary makes one critical mistake: not 88% of the securities accepted as marketable assets by the Central Bank are in breach of the Charter of Fundamental Rights, instead 88% of the 29,552 securities accepted by the ECB at the time of the study in 2017 were subject to an examination as only these were found in the data set provided by Oekom Research AG (now part of Institutional Shareholder Services Inc.). Accordingly, 26,110 securities were examined regarding to human rights controversies (e.g. child labour or forced labour), controversial environmental behavior and controversial economic practices (e.g. corruption & questionable handling of tax liability). The sustainability rating agency uses an operationalization based on international conventions and guidelines as a yardstick for determining which behavior is considered controversial in this sense. Only serious and very serious controversies were taken into account when assessing and classifying companies and countries. The number of securities showing serious controversies in business conduct was 4751 regarding tax payments, 2023 regarding monetary transactions, 247 regarding corruption, 181 regarding environmental destruction, 70 regarding human rights violations and and 10 regarding the production of outlawed weapons. In the business conduct of suppliers/financiers regarding human rights violations 8 securities with serious controversies were found in connection with child labor and 7 in connection with forced labor. The number is not based on issuers, but on the number of securities that show these controversies. Thus, several securities of an issuer with controversies are also counted several times. In addition, it should be noted that particularly questionable companies have several types of controversies, so that the numbers cannot simply be summed up. After further controversy screenings in the ongoing handling of the petition—including an IMUG rating with data from Vigeo Eiris (www.imug.de/imug-rating-english)—it became apparent, that around one fifth of all securities in the list of marketable assets are subject to one or more serious controversies.

At no time was the Committee on Petitions' summary questioned by any political actors. The supposed controversies regarding the Charter of Fundamental Rights in "up to 88% of companies," is clearly not plausible because of the immense number, but was never questioned. The European Commission itself does not at all seem to be disturbed by the alarmingly high (due to the false summary) percentage. What could be the reasons for this? Perhaps it is due to low diligence, lack of understanding, even apathy towards an almost completely unethical financial market or simply as a lack of interest in the results.

2.2 *Barely Acceptable*

On May 15th, 2017 the petition was registered under the number 0429/2017 entitled "Compliance of the European Central Bank with the EU Charter of Fundamental Rights." It was formally examined and then found worthy of consideration by the Committee on Petitions at its meeting in Brussels on October 11th, 2017. At that time, the Committee on Petitions considered the topic to be so important that it was referred to individually on the Committee's website: "Petitions on economic and monetary affairs—Debate: 11.10.2017 27-09-2017—12:13 PETI Members will debate a series of petitions regarding economic and monetary affairs, in particular the activities and policies of the European Central Bank (ECB). Petitions from Spain, France, and Germany raise the issues of ECB transparency, low-interest rate policy, decision-making procedures, and the compliance of ECB practices with the EU Charter of Fundamental Rights." I was very pleased at the time and my confidence in the institutions of our European Union grew. However, the conditions for the debate in the committee were extremely poor. The petition was mixed in with monetary policy concerns on low interest rate policy and other issues. Inexplicably, the petition was summarized with a totally inappropriate further petition, as was apparent from the agenda published. Since I was unable to be present in Brussels that day and had previously informed the committee accordingly, it was not possible for me to make corrections on the spot.

Committee Chair Cecilia Wikström (Group of the Alliance of Liberals and Democrats for Europe, Sweden) wanted to close the petition together with other petitions quickly. She had forgotten to initiate a debate voicing my concerns, which was only made up for by the intervention of Notis Marias (Member of the Bureau of the Group of the European Conservatives and Reformers, Greece). One can get the impression that the absence of the petitioner had been used strategically to let the matter fall asleep quickly and quietly. On the other hand, it was already later than expected and the meeting participants were, perhaps, a little tired as the topics were dealt with at the end of the meeting. In my opinion the representatives of the European Commission also gave the impression, by their lack of reaction, that an undisputed closure of the petition may be in their interest. In the following statements the representatives of the European Commission made it clear that they fully understood that the ECB's conduct was aimed at preventing violations of fundamental rights. In this context, however, they unequivocally and emphatically took the view that this issue was part of the ECB's monetary policy and that the ECB needs to act independently regarding such conduct. The European Commission respects the independence of the ECB. I watched the meeting live on the Internet in a business ethics forum that I co-organized. When I heard these words in that particular context, I couldn't believe my ears. It seemed to me as if the European Commission's definition of the ECB's independence was meant to legitimize the ECB's possible violation of fundamental rights and human rights. Again, the chairwoman of the committee wanted to close the petition after the comment of the representative of the European Commission. However, Notis Marias, who was very attentive despite a long day of meetings, spoke out against this once again. He pointed out that violation of the EU Charter of Fundamental Rights is a central issue for the European Parliament. The petition should therefore be kept open and the ECB (Mario Dragi) should first be asked to comment on the matter. Only then did the chairwoman give in. It was announced that the petition would be kept open and that the committee would send a letter to the ECB. At the beginning of December 2017, the Committee on Petitions wrote to me to announce that it would seek additional opinions: from the ECB itself and an update from the European Commission. In addition, the Parliamentary Committee on Economic and Monetary Affairs was also asked to make a comment.

2.3 Patience

In order to provide all political actors involved with an up-to-date basis for decision-making and the same level of information, the study was updated, and the reasoning summarized in a way to foster easy comprehension. On January 4th, 2018 the document, written in German, (see Annex A.2) was sent to:

- European Parliament, Committee on Economic and Monetary Affairs, Chairman Roberto Gualtieri
- European Commission, Directorate-General Justice and Consumers, Commissioner Věra Jourová; Directorate-General Financial Stability, Services and Capital Market Union, Vice-President Valdis Dombrovskis; Directorate-General Economic and Financial Affairs/Directorate-General Taxation and Customs Union, Commissioner Pierre Moscovici; Directorate-General Competition Policy, Commissioner Margrethe Vestager.
- European Central Bank, President Mario Draghi

A copy was sent at the same time to

- European Parliament, Committee on Petitions, Chairwoman Cecilia Wikström; Committee member Notis Marias
- All political group chairmen in the European Parliament
- European Union Agency for Fundamental Rights

At the beginning of March 2018, there was still no feedback from the Committee on Petitions or the responsible bodies, and the issue still had not been discussed anywhere in the EU's strategic vision finding for a sustainable financial market. On March 5th 2018, Ms. Wikström received a reminder in the following form: "Three months ago, you promised to obtain information on the facts of Petition 0429/2017. Two months ago, I updated the supporting documents for the petition and sent them to you and the relevant bodies. On February 2nd, 2018, Molly Scott Cato presented the draft report on sustainable finance (2018/2007(INI)) to the Committee on Economic and Monetary Affairs. It reads in paragraph 19: Calls on the ECB to restructure its purchase programs in order to refocus its portfolio and align it with an investment strategy consistent with the Paris Convention and the ESG objectives. However, the draft does not contain a word on compliance with the EU Charter of Fundamental Rights of ECB purchase programs and of ECB acceptance of marketable assets. I would be very grateful if you could let me know about the status of feedback and further steps in the policy-making process, as decisions on sustainable finance can hardly have any real effect without the implementation of the point raised in petition 0429/2017. How can I help to ensure that petition 0429/2017 is explicitly included in the proposal for a decision on sustainable finance and that it is sent to all parliamentarians and commissioners to form their opinion in advance?"

On March 7th the ECON Committee's opinion (see Sect. 2.4) on the petition was sent as a reply, although it was only made available in English and did not address any of the questions raised in the petition. I decided that it would make sense to change all future communication to English and I decided to translate the updated summary from January 4th, 2018 as follows:

"Summary and update of petition 0429/2017 to the European Parliament: European Central Bank (ECB) involved in a massive number of violations of the Charter of Fundamental Rights of the European Union through possession and trading of unethical securities

Ladies and gentlemen,

you were asked by the European Parliament's Committee on Petition 0429/2017 for an opinion. To make this easier for you, I have summarized the facts and attached an update of my study::

Circumstances

The ECB is playing a major role in undermining the most fundamental values of the European Union by accepting questionable securities as collateral for its monetary policy operations. The effects of this action have a significant influence on the development of the European Union due to its large transaction volume. Therefore, the ECB and its agents must refrain from trading in and holding securities related to infringements of the Charter of Fundamental Rights of the European Union.

4781 Banks and savings banks were obliged in the euro area in 2017 to hold minimum reserve assets with the ECB (or its national central bank). A further 2493 financial institutions and funds were listed business partners of the ECB for refinancing operations. This meant that 7274 banks, savings banks, money market funds and financial institutions, including national central banks, were obliged to hold so-called eligible collateral for monetary policy transactions with the ECB in their portfolios. The traded volume of these securities currently stands at around 14 trillion € and is thus a major lever for or against the realisation of European values in the real economy. The ECB (or the respective national central bank as vicarious agent) becomes the owner of the relevant securities as a pledgee eligible collateral. Trade in and possession of securities which undermine the Charter of Fundamental Rights of the European Union is detrimental to the European Union. For a European institution such as the ECB, this is unacceptable and cannot be justified by independence in monetary policy.

Supporting Documents

The ECB's website provides access to its daily updated list of marketable collateral accepted as collateral for monetary policy operations (= marketable eligible collateral). In addition, there are also unpublished, non-marketable securities that meet the eligibility criteria and are accepted as collateral. The marketable securities of all issuers meeting the central bank eligibility criteria on January 3, 2018 were examined by the independent sustainability rating agency oekom research AG (oekom) on January 4, 2018 with daily ratings. Of the 29,445 securities, 25,111 were examined with daily ratings, which corresponds to a coverage ratio of 85%. Once again, the investigation focused only on serious and very serious ethical controversies of the aspects of the EU Charter of Fundamental Rights, which were examined in 2017 (Article 32 Child Labour; Article 37 Environmental Protection; Article 5 Violations of human rights, such as forced labour; tax avoidance and corruption). The audit again revealed the following alarming results (and thus an increase in infringements):

Type of controversy/number of securities in the ECB register of marketable collateral:

Serious controversies in business conduct regarding …

Tax payments 4481 securities
Cash transactions 1592 securities
Corruption 936 securities
Environmental protection 1480 securities
Human rights violations 72 securities
Production of outlawed weapons 16 securities

Remedy

In order to remedy the deplorable state of affairs simply and effectively, the permanent non-infringement of the EU Charter of Fundamental Rights must be included in the criteria for eligible collateral as a condition for admission. Compliance with the EU Charter of Fundamental Rights is regularly verified by a current ethical rating. In terms of competition policy, the ethical rating can be transparently mapped by means of the independent ethical ratings already available on the market from established rating agencies to which the ECB and all other financial market players have access at all times.

Reasons
The existence of the EU Charter of Fundamental Rights implies a natural obligation for the ECB to proceed as proposed above. Since my analysis of marketable central bank eligible collateral has revealed mass violations of the Charter of Fundamental Rights of the European Union, explicit inclusion of this European minimum morality in the ECB's statutes is urgently needed. To date, the ECB and the European financial market have not been sufficient to enforce the Charter of Fundamental Rights of the European Union."

This translation, together with the following cover letter in German and English, was sent to the Petitions Committee and the ECON Committee as well as to all actors listed above on 7.3.2018: "Dear PETI secretariat, dear ECON committee, thank you for your message today. I am aware of the information provided by Roberto Gualtieri. I watch this topics regularly. There must be a misunderstanding, because the answer given by Roberto Gualtieri has nothing to do with the specific and fundamental questions of my petition. It does not answer any of the petition's questions. To be on the safe side, I would like to add the summary of my concern, which is extremely important to the European Union, here in English again. I hope that this will lead to the ECON Committee and Mr Gualtieri actually reading the matter and responding precisely to these points."

At the beginning of April, Susanne Bergius had interviewed an ECB spokesman and me about the petition for the *Handelsblatt Business Briefing Sustainable Investments*. (See Handelsblatt Business Briefing Sustainable Investments No. 4 of 13.04.2018, p. 7 ff.) The information provided by the ECB spokesman to Susanne Bergius shows that the petition, with its simple purpose, was either not read in full or not understood at all, or that the expected response from the ECB was aimed at not making any concrete changes. The article by Susanne Bergius was partially translated into English by me and sent on April 16th, 2018 to the relevant authorities for their consideration—also to the president of the ECB himself—in order to be able to revise the reply to the Committee on Petitions once again:

Petition: EU Parliament on the Move
Per request the ECB said that it would inform the Chairman of the Committee on Petitions in the coming weeks. However they also stated, "It is difficult to answer in more detail, because the petition does not give concrete examples of securities of which it claims that they are contrary to the Charter of European Human Rights [sic!]. the petition only mentions Numbers." Obviously the spokesman had not read the petition thoroughly, otherwise he would have noticed names like Anheuser-Busch, Airbus, Eni, Ferrovial, Lafarge, JP Morgan Chase and Wells Fargo […] There's a lot more and even harder cases,' says Bolsinger. Deutsche Bank's papers would fill books.

The ECB further complains that the petition appears to mix collateral and minimum reserves. It establishes a link between a bank's obligation to minimum reserve requirements and requirements of securities for refinancing operations. Bolsinger replies: "The petition addresses both issues [...]. If the first part, abolishing the acceptance of unethical collateral is fulfilled, the second part is not necessary, because then the commercial banks have no incentives/obligations to hold unethical papers."

With regard to the possibility of including environmental, social and governance criteria (ESG), the ECB spokesperson emphasized that it is fully in line with the current regulation. It also supports efforts to find the best ways to challenges such as global warming. For example, it contributes to the G20 Green Finance Study Group. This deals with how the financial system could help stimulate private green investments.

ECB Does Not Observe ESG Criteria

Apart from this, however, the ECB believes that it is first and foremost a matter of political and economic policy decision-makers to come to an agreement and to implement relevant laws and measures in order to achieve ethical, ecological or other goals. "The ECB does not currently apply such criteria, because there is a lack of a well-defined framework for so-called ESG criteria based on broad approval," said the spokesperson. While there are striking examples of unethical activities of companies, there are many areas of activity where it is not clear what is morally or socially acceptable. "In any case it is not primarily up to the ECB to define this, but to the legislator."

This argument has three weak points: if this were the case, there would be no need for an institutional investor to look after ESG, as neither the EU nor most national legislators directly prescribe something in this regard. [...] Secondly, the ECB argument does not match the words of its President Mario Draghi, it also has to act in the sense of sustainability goals [...]. Third, the legislator has already acted through the EU Charter of Fundamental Rights—it also applies to the ECB. "The legislator must now pass implementing legislation or regulations to ensure that the ECB fulfils its obligations" Bolsinger demands.

The Legislator Seems to Be in Charge

That is why I filed the petition. "It seems to me that this straightforward topic is a too hot potato for many people: The simple question is whether the ECB is above the EU Charter of Fundamental Rights, and thus basically all democratically legitimized decisions can be levered by their monetary policy. We issue environmental protection regulations, but the ECB promotes the financing of environmental degradation, and so on..."

On April 25th, 2018 at 15:23 a memo of the entire mailing list was given with a translation of the article on the petition that had meanwhile appeared in the German newspaper *taz:* "Subject: "European Central Bank (ECB) involved in a massive number of violations of the Charter of Fundamental Rights of the European Union."

Dear Mrs. Wikström, ladies and gentlemen,

some time ago you tried to obtain information on the facts of Petition 0429/2017. The feedback is still outstanding—I would be pleased if you could remind those asked of their feedback, because in the meantime the press itself is seeking information—e.g. directly from the ECB. I have attached another exemplary article of the German "taz" with the statements of the ECB as an English translation."

The secretariat of the Committee on Petitions replied on 26 April:: "prior to proceeding with further treatment of your petition the response from the European Central Bank is awaited. A reminder will be sent in due time if no timely response is received." On 26 June 2018 ECBs official reply to the Committee on Petitions (see Chap. 2), was passed on to me with the announcement of the secretariat of the Committee on Petitions that I will be informed by the Chair of the Petitions Committee on the further processing of the petition in due course.

The next day, I informed the Committee on Petitions that the ECB did not provide concrete answers to the simple questions of the petition either: "Dear Mrs Wikström, Ladies and gentlemen, there must be a misunderstanding in the ECB, too. Because the letter of the ECB does not answer any of the petition's simple questions. I am really curious about what you will decide to do next on the facts, that no one gave answers that you or the parliament can work with. Please find enclosed a copy of my letters to MEPs, that the ECB cited in their answer to you."

Five months later I asked the Petitions Committee about the status of the petition, as I was to present the contents and status of petition 0429/2017 at an event of the Hub4Sustainable Finance Germany. As feedback, I received an updated but in content unchanged reply from the European Commission to petition 0429/2017 on 20 September 2019 (see Chap. 2) with the note, I would be informed by letter of the Chair of the Committee on Petitions once the Committee has reached a decision on the further processing of the petition.

The contents of the petition presented in Hub4Sustainable Finance Germany were later adopted by the German Council for Sustainable Development in its statement of 15.10.2019 for the Federal Government "The Federal Government's Sustainable Finance Strategy must break new ground". Point 10 calls for a regulation of the ECB in the sense of this petition. The Council goes beyond the existing fundamental rights obligation and even calls for the "ECB to be bound by the principle of sustainability"! The German Sustainable Finance Advisory Board has also extended its "Living Document" to include this point.

On 31 January 2019, when no activity on the part of the Petitions Committee was discernible for a further four months, the Chairmen of the Petitions Committee again got a reminder: "Dear Ladies & Gentlemen, in the Committee on Petitions Meetings on 21 January 2019 and 22 January 2019 the petition 0429/2017 again was not on the topic list, but you have submitted the excellent "OPINION of the Committee on Petitions for the Committee on Constitutional Affairs on the implementation of the Charter of Fundamental Rights of the European Union in the EU institutional framework (2017/2089(INI))". Herein you "reiterate strongly that the EU institutions need to respect the Charter under all circumstances and in whichever role they play", but again 4 months have passed without any message and action on your part on the petition 0429/2017. It is doubtless, that the ECB as institution has to comply with the Charter of Fundamental Rights of the European Union and must not promote fundamental rights violations by promoting and possessing assets of criminals themselves. Discrimination, slavery, environmental destruction, exploitation of people & white-collar crime will never be reduced in EU, when the ECB makes the financial system accept all that and when they even accept and support it themselves by buying assets from proven and sentenced criminals. If you really are interested in clarifying this fundamental issue for the EU, you would have to insist on an answer from the ECB-President himself to the simple questions enclosed in my petition. To react and communicate to the honorable Committee on Petitions like the ECB did with its ridiculous and meaningless answer written by PR staff shows in my opinion, how the ECB seems to feel: rulers beyond the Charter without the duty to be accountable to parliament and the people. Especially when there will soon be change in ECB-Presidency, the new president should be aware, that the European Parliament will have an eye on this fundamental point and therefore you should urge the ECB-President for a qualified answer."

The PETI Secretariat answered on 7.2.2019: "Please note that the agenda-setting of the Petitions Committee is determined according to the requests and political priorities of the Members of the Committee. As such, the petitions which figure on the monthly agenda are grouped and selected by the Secretariat in response to such requests. Any actions taken in relation to the further processing of a petition must reflect decisions taken during a Committee meeting. With regards to your petition 0429/2017, it has already figured on the agenda of the meeting of 11–12 October 2017. Since then, the Committee has requested and obtained three written responses from the European Commission, as well as the response from the European Central Bank, which have all been transmitted to you. In addition, the petition has been transmitted to the Committee on Economic and Monetary Affairs. The Secretariat can only take further action or send correspondence in relation to a petition following a decision being taken by the Committee. Should your petition be added to a future agenda, you will be duly informed thereof, as well as of any follow-up action taken thereafter."

2.4 Overview of Official Answers

2.4.1 European Commission

The opinion of the European Commission delivered in 2017 at the first meeting of the Committee on Petitions was published in the Notice to Members of the Committee on Petitions of 13.08.2018 (see CM\1160720EN.docx PE615.346v03-00):

"Petition 0429/2017 relates to the conduct of monetary policy in the euro area, and in particular to the ECB's minimum reserve requirements and the acceptance of assets by the ECB. The Commission respects the ECB's exclusive competence and independence in the pursuit of its monetary policy, in line with the TFEU. Therefore, the Commission is not in a position to comment on questions regarding the extent to which the ECB has to ensure that the provisions of the EU Charter of Fundamental Rights are taken into account when conducting and carrying out monetary policy.

Conclusion: The Commission cannot take further action as the petitions are related to policy areas where the ECB has exclusive competence and is granted independence by the TFEU. The petitions should be addressed to the ECB. Moreover, it has to be kept in mind that the ECB is accountable for its policies, including through regular reporting and dialogue with the European Parliament (Article 284 TFEU)."

On November 11, 2019 in Brussels I replied to this comment and made quite clear that no EU institution is independent of the Fundamental Rights Charter. Therefore, the Commission could, at the very least, define eligibility criteria guidelines for compliance with the EU Fundamental Rights. Secondly, petitions are a matter for the Petition Committee. In their answer, the ECB urges political authorities (= the petition committee) to "define, agree and promote" ethical minimum standards to implement in their everyday work. It is not the ECB itself that can make decisions regarding the actions of the Petition Committee. It should become standard procedure that the ECB reports on fundamental rights compliance to the Parliament regularly according to the accountability that the Commission cites. This has never happened in the entirety of the EU's history! Respecting fundamental rights does not violate the institutional independence of the ECB, it is not political instruction and is not a matter of exclusive competence on monetary policy! The Commission has not yet changed their reply.

2.4.2 ECON Committee

The reply was sent to the Chairman of the Committee on Petitions on March 7th, 2018 and was subsequently brought directly to my attention as the petitioner: "D 303868, 07.03.2018, ASP08G201

Subject: Petition No 0429/2017 by Harald Bolsinger (German) on the compliance of the European Central Bank with the EU Charter of Fundamental Rights

Dear Ms Wikstrom,

Thank you for transmitting petition No 0429/2017 to the Committee on Economic and Monetary Affairs for information. ECON examined the petition and we confirm monetary policies fall within the competence of our Committee which is tasked to implement the accountability of the European Central Bank to the European Parliament.

ECON Committee has repeatedly called the ECB to increase the transparency of its monetary policy framework, with a particular focus in the recent period on the Corporate Sector Purchase Programme (CSPP) which enables the Eurosystem to purchase bonds issued by non-bank corporations domiciled in the euro area. In the view of these calls, the ECB has started publishing substantially more details on the CSPP. The petitioner could usefully refer to the information published on our website regarding the Quarterly Monetary Dialogues between the ECB President and the ECON Committee (http://www.europarl.europa.eu/committees/en/econ/monetary-dialogue.html), to the ECB website detailing the information on the CSPP, including the list of securities held (https://www.ecb.europa.eu/mopo/implement/omt/html/index.en.html#cspp) and to the annual reports voted by the European Parliament on the ECB annual report. The last report published is on the ECB 2015 annual report with rapporteur Ramon Tremosa I Balcells.

I would suggest informing the petitioner along the lines of this letter.

Yours sincerely,

Roberto Gualtieri"

I informed Roberto Gualtieri of the ECON committee by e-mail on the same day that his answers did not address the petition's questions at any point and expected a further statement to the Committee on Petitions containing comments on the petition's factual questions instead of a reference to sources that do not provide any information on the subject of fundamental rights compliance. On March 7, 2018 at 20:26:16 Mr. Gualtieri sent a "read" confirmation to this e-mail—but again, I have not received a reply.

2.4.3 ECB

On June 26, 2018, the ECB's official reply of June 22, 2018 to the Committee on Petitions was received: "Re: Petition No 0429/2017 by Harald Bolsinger (German) on the compliance of the European Central Bank with the EU Charter of Fundamental Rights

> Honourable Member of the European Parliament, dear Ms Wikstrom,
>
> Thank you for your letter informing the European Central Bank (ECB) about the discussion held by the Committee on Petitions of the European Parliament. The ECB's President, Mario Draghi, had the opportunity to discuss the issues raised by the petitioner in both the regular hearings before the European Parliament's Committee on Economic and Monetary Affairs and in published replies to a significant number of written questions from Members of the European Parliament (MEPs). In particular, in the reply letter to Ms Lynn Boylan dated 11 May 2017, he clarified that the ECB's primary objective, as mandated by the Treaty on the Functioning of the European Union, is to ensure price stability over the medium term. The eligibility of assets for our monetary policy operations is thus primarily guided by our monetary policy objective and appropriate financial risk management considerations. Further remarks made more recently by the ECB President regarding the issues raised by the petitioner can be found in other written replies to MEPs, including in the letter to Ms Laura Agea and Mr Marco Valli dated 23 January 2018. The ECB's collateral policy was also recently discussed in the ECB feedback on the input provided by the European Parliament as part of its resolution on the ECB Annual Report for 2016,3 which explains that a broad set of eligible collateral helps to ensure that monetary policy is implemented smoothly and effectively. The document also clarifies that the Eurosystem has in place a detailed set of requirements relating to the eligibility and use of assets as collateral, as well as a detailed set of risk control measures applied to collateral. These requirements and measures are publicly available, and the ECB publishes the list of marketable assets which are eligible as collateral on a daily basis. In relation to the specific issues of environmental protection that the petitioner raised, I would refer you to the ECB President's comments in his written answer to several MEPs dated 11 April 2017.4 The ECB recognizes the great importance of climate-related issues to our societies and believes that, in the first instance, it is up to political authorities to define, agree and promote appropriate measures to address such issues. In this sense, the ECB welcomes the European Commission's action plan on financing sustainable growth of 8 March 2017, which is a plan for a greener and cleaner

economy. The ECB supports the political efforts to develop a common EU taxonomy of sustainable assets, as well as the proposals for strengthening sustainability disclosure. The ECB also participates in various international and European fora (e.g. the G20, the Financial Stability Board and the European Systemic Risk Board), where implications and challenges arising from climate change and climate change-related policies are discussed, and supports the ongoing work to identify the best way forward on this important global challenge. As an example of global work in this regard, the ECB contributes to the G20 Green Finance Study Group, which is investigating how to enhance the ability of the financial system to mobilise private capital for green investment. Moreover, the ECB recently joined the Network for Greening the Financial System, which brings together central banks and supervisors committed to developing common supervisory and macroprudential practices to address climate-related and environmental risks. Finally, the ECB's Vice-President, Vitor Constancio, stated to the Committee on Economic and Monetary Affairs on 9 April 2018 that, despite the absence of an explicit climate-related target in the ECB's purchases under the extended asset purchase programme (APP), the programme has made a positive contribution to funding climate-related projects through its purchases of green bonds in monetary policy portfolios. This issue has also been recently discussed in a letter of reply to several MEPs dated 12 June 2018. I hope these actions have adequately highlighted the extent to which the ECB has already presented its views on the fulfilment of its mandate to the European Parliament and MEPs."

In this reply, the ECB has consciously committed itself to the broadest possible portfolio of marketable assets for which monetary policy objectives and financial risk aspects are primarily relevant from the ECB's perspective. At the same time, the answer reveals that the ECB is well aware of the impact of its bond purchase programs. The letter points out that if the ECB buys good (green) bonds, they also have good (green) effects. Conversely, this means that the ECB is well aware that by buying unethical bonds it also promotes unethical effects and seemingly accepts this!

On June 27th 2018, I drew the attention of all parliamentarians named in the letter of the ECB to the petition by fax, each with a copy to the Committee on Petitions. The individual fax content showed the ECB's present opinion and the misrepresentations of Mario Draghi. A further reaction from the ECB during Mario Draghi's term of office did not occur.

The Lisbon Treaties make the EU Charter of Fundamental Rights a directly applicable primary law in all European institutions. All the ECB's operations as a European institution must therefore comply with the codified values of the Charter of Fundamental Rights. The above shows, that the ECB is aware of the effects of their assets purchase programs and collateral eligibility: they talk about positive effects by buying good (ecological) assets and therefore know about the negative effects as well. The ECB's response to the petition shows that it is waiting for political action- it even asks for regulation in its reply!

2.5 *A Wind of Change*

Evasive and long-awaited answers from the Petitions Committee of the European Parliament for the 2014-2019 parliamentary terms gave the impression that there's a poor perspective for the future of fundamental rights in the European financial market. The report on the work of this committee does not contain anything on the subject either (see www.europarl.europa.eu/RegData/etudes/STUD/2019/621917/IPOL_STU(2019)621917_EN.pdf). The Committee on Petitions of the new parliamentary term, on the other hand, put the issue on the agenda as soon as its business began. On September 11th, 2019 I asked the PETI Secretariat again about the planned follow-up action and when the new committee will start its work. On October 3rd, 2019 I was informed that the petition is on the Committees' Agenda for November 11th, 2019. The new Committee on Petitions is chaired by Dolors Montserrat.

In its meeting in Brussels on November 11th, 2019 I had the chance to explain the main points of the petition again. After an exciting debate in response to my explanations the confusing link to the completely inappropriate further petition that was made by the old Committee on Petitions in the meeting in May 2017 was cancelled on that day. Three favorable opinions from parliamentarians on the petition's core issue were submitted: by Jude Kirton-Darling (Progressive Alliance of Social Democrats) of the United Kingdom and by the two Germans Ulrike Müller (Renew Europe Group) and Peter Jahr (Group of the European People's Party). The other petition was subsequently closed and the "fundamental rights petition 429/2017" was kept open, with the intention of discussing ECB obligations for fundamental rights compliance with the newly constituted decision makers and the new ECB president. On January 14th 2020, I received a message from Dolors Montserrat, that the Committee again decided to send a letter to the European Central Bank. On April 28th, 2020, I asked the Petitions Committee what the state of affairs was like. They sent a copy of the letter to Ms Lagarde on May 27th, 2020 as an answer. The letter was sent to the President of the European Central Bank on January 14th, 2020. In May, according to the Committee on Petitions, she received also a reminder by e-mail with a request for a reply. The committee will continue the examination of the petition as soon as it has received the necessary information from the ECB. Therefore, there is a real opportunity to counter the ethical blindness of the Eurosystem politically in the current parliamentary term.

3 Summary and Outlook: Opportunity for a Global Paradigm Shift

The opportunity for European citizens to file petitions is undoubtedly a wonderful achievement of the EU. The basic claim of the Petition 0429/2017 is that the ECB—and Europe—urgently need clear exclusionary criteria for assets accepted as collateral and for the asset purchase programs of the ECB with the goal to not undermine the European values of the Charter of Fundamental Rights. The European Commission should define those exclusionary criteria for the ECB based on the EU Charter of Fundamental Rights together with the EU Parliament which has to monitor the compliance regularly as guardian of the Charter of Fundamental Rights.

Never before in the history of the EU has the Central Bank provided Parliament with transparency on the fundamental rights compliance of its portfolios, although transparency and credible communication in all areas are the most important elements of successful central banking action. A first step in the right direction would be the political demand on the part of the EU Parliament to publicly establish this transparency. Then, in a second step the Commission should develop measures for bonds and securities within the existing regulatory framework with the goal to exclude companies violating fundamental rights from all portfolios of the ECB and the national central banks.

It is a stroke of luck that the proceedings of this petition lasted from 2017 to 2019, as there is now a real chance of change by new leaders and decision-makers at the right levels. The new ECB president has the unique opportunity to make Europe's central bank a role model for all central banks worldwide and to provide the EU Parliament with a lasting picture of the relevance of European core values in the central bank's core business on the basis of reliable data. The elimination of the ECB's ethical blindness can be implemented immediately by discrimination of unethical assets in the sense of the EU Charter of Fundamental Rights. While many steps of a green deal in Europe still require additional regulation, the ECB can start immediately. The Golden Calf of a supposedly ethically blind Eurosystem would thus have been knocked off its pedestal once and for all. If the ECB does not implement this and the European Commission tolerates a failure to act, it is possible to take legal action. But that would be unworthy of Europe…

Sources:

https://europa.eu
https://www.right-basedonscience.de/en
https://www.imug.de/imug-rating-english/ http://www.issgovernance.com/esg/
http://www.wirtschaftsethik.biz/centralbank
Handelsblatt Bussiness Briefing Sustainable Investments No. 4 of 13.04.2018

On the Role of the ECB in Sustainable Finance

Michael Schmidt

Abstract The ECB has successfully performed its main task in the context of an independent monetary policy: The euro is stable and enjoys the confidence of the population and the economy. Regarding sustainability, the ECB has so far displayed varying degrees of ambition. The ECB on its own can, and should, expand its commitment within its mandate. By contrast, any attempt by politicians or corporates to exercise undue influence would end up in a loss of stability and prosperity.

1 Article

The European Central Bank is the logical continuation of the Bundesbank in the euro area. As the guardian of the D-mark, the Bundesbank played a large part in ensuring the economic stability of the Federal Republic of Germany by pursuing a reliable and politically independent monetary policy. As a result, the Bundesbank has enjoyed a high level of trust in large parts of the population and the economy. The institution is still a highly esteemed authority in the financial system. However, the introduction of the euro and the substitution of the D-mark required a different institution in 1998 to manage the new currency for all countries of the monetary union.

The objective of the Eurosystem, that includes the ECB and the national central banks of the euro countries, is defined in Art. 127 of the TFEU *(Treaty on the Functioning of the European Union)*: "The primary objective of the European System of Central Banks *(ESCB)* shall be to maintain price stability." In addition to its monetary policy mandate, the ECB also is the supervisor of the significant credit institutions in the euro area. In Germany, it hence supplements the Bundesbank's supervisory function for smaller, less significant institutions.

M. Schmidt (✉)
Member of the Executive Board and Chief Investment Officer of Lloyd Fonds AG, Member of the Sustainable Finance Committee of the German government, Member of the High Level Expert Group on Sustainable Finance of the European Commission, Lloyd Fonds AG, Hamburg, Germany
e-mail: michael.schmidt@lloydfonds.de

H. Bolsinger et al. (eds.), *The European Central Bank as a Sustainability Role Model*, Sustainable Finance, https://doi.org/10.1007/978-3-030-55450-7_4

To evaluate the ECB's record in monetary policy, capital market observers typically use two benchmarks that reflect the trust a currency enjoys:

1. The performance and the purchasing power of the euro;
2. The importance of the euro as a reserve currency.

The value of the euro has proven to be stable during the last 20 years, with fluctuations not unusual for freely floating exchange rates. According to OECD figures, the purchasing power of the euro has increased by 16% against the US dollar since its introduction in 2018. Price stability is another indicator of the euro's soundness. During the last 20 years, inflation in the euro area was 1.7% on average. This means that the ECB has clearly achieved its aim of keeping inflation rates at below, but close to 2%. Meanwhile, the euro, as a reserve currency, has become an indispensable, and increasing part of the foreign exchange reserves of many central banks outside of the Eurozone. According to the IMF, some 20% of the world's currency reserves were denominated in euros in the second quarter of 2019. Although the euro's share is smaller than the US dollar's, which amounts to 60%, it is larger by far than that of the British Pound or the Japanese Yen, each of which only account for roughly 5%.

In summary, the analysis of the two criteria proves the great trust in the euro, which is also reflected by surveys among citizens of the euro area; according to a survey conducted by the European Commission at the end of 2018, almost two-thirds of the respondents were in favour of the euro. The approval rating in Germany was even as high as 70%.

This means that the ECB has successfully and responsibly performed its principal task of ensuring price stability. In this respect, it is of fundamental importance that its independence is safeguarded. Any attempt by politicians or corporations to exercise undue influence would end up in a loss of stability and prosperity.

Against that background, what role does the ECB play in the transformation process towards a sustainable financial system? As a member of the Network for Greening the Financial System (NGFS), it does not elude the sustainable finance dynamics [1].

However, because of its mandate described above, the ECB is cautious to add emphasis here. Trust is key to the stability of a currency, indeed, of the financial system as a whole. Hence, confidence-building monetary policy is a great responsibility. Due to this responsibility, the ECB cannot, on the one hand, improvidently yield to political demands and activism. On the other hand, the progress made in designing a sustainable financial system and a sustainable economy is not just a political process. Climate change is a physical fact. Thus, a central bank also needs to deal with it and develop measures that suit the institution. A few national central banks have already reinterpreted their mandate accordingly, with the Bank of England and the Dutch National Bank being among the pioneers.

The ECB's regulatory framework actually gives it sufficient scope for autonomously broadening the interpretation of its mandate. The TFEU provides: "Without prejudice to the objective of price stability, the ESCB shall support the general economic policies in the Union with a view to contributing to the achievement of the objectives of the Union as laid down in Article 3 of the Treaty on European Union." In addition to economic growth, price stability and employment, Article 3 of the EU treaty also lays down environmental, social and ethical objectives. This means:

price stability is the dominant goal. However, if it is not impaired, the ECB can and shall also support the other objectives of the EU.

So far, the ECB has addressed sustainability issues in its three areas of responsibility

1. banking supervision;
2. financial stability; and
3. monetary policy, including market operations.

In the areas of banking supervision and financial stability, the ECB definitely proceeds ambitiously, not least because of its collaboration in the NGFS. The ECB clearly considers it its duty to participate in the development of indicators and stress tests in order to improve climate-related risk assessment and to indicate to the institutions supervised by it how they should handle climate-related risks. In 2019, it has rated climate-related risks among the key risk drivers of the Eurozone's banking system.

As part of its Asset Purchase Programme, the ECB also includes green bonds on its list of eligible assets for monetary policy. The ECB is careful, however, to buy green bonds only in proportion to their share of the overall bond market, so as to avoid a prejudice for certain types of bonds and to maintain market neutrality.

The ECB can, should, and probably will expand its commitment to sustainability. Yet, additional players and measures in the financial industry are of fundamental importance in order to achieve the Sustainable Development Goals (SDGs) adopted by the world community with an overwhelming majority in 2015 and the targets of the Paris Agreement (to limit global warming to a maximum of 1.5–2 degrees Celsius by 2050). The most important driver of the accelerating dynamics in sustainable finance is the European Commission's ten-point action plan "Financing Sustainable Growth" adopted in 2018, which is largely based on the trend-setting final report of the European Commission's High Level Expert Group on Sustainable Finance (HLEG). The HLEG final report does not include a recommendation on the ECB or monetary policy more generally because it was not part of the assignment respecting the ECB's independence.

The EU action plan aims to:

1. Reorient capital flows towards sustainable investment in order to achieve sustainable and inclusive growth;
2. Manage financial risks stemming from climate change, resource depletion, environmental degradation and social issues; and
3. Foster transparency and long termism in financial and economic activity.

This means that the European Commission wishes the financial system to play a comprehensive role. Not only is the financial industry targeted to help close the funding gap for achieving the sustainable development goals and climate objectives, given its capital allocation and multiplier function. The financial system is to become sustainable altogether: a more long-term orientation, a broader risk awareness and social usefulness shall become its characteristics. This is finally the opportunity to regain the trust lost during the financial crisis.

However, the HLEG's final report also has highlighted that although the financial industry plays a key role, a completely coordinated approach to sustainable development is required, one that aligns changes in the financial system with economic policy. Of particular concern here are reliable policy frameworks (such as an exit date for coal), efficient price signals for internalising external effects (e.g. via an adequate price on carbon emissions) and the elimination of inconsistencies in financial regulation (e.g. the potential overemphasis on short-term liquidity that conflicts with many long-term sustainability investments). In the end, the financial system is only the link between those providing capital and those in need of capital. To actually achieve sustainability objectives, capital allocation must eventually take effect in products, services and production processes, i.e. throughout the economy and in consumption patterns.

Europe is well placed to take a leading position at the global level in the transformation of the economic and financial system towards more sustainability, not least in the sense of creating a growth-oriented competitive advantage. Europe's willingness to do so has become more tangible as evidenced by the international platform for sustainable finance launched in October 2019 and by the Green Deal of the new European Commission.

As a final thought, there should be less worry about too little sustainability at the ECB, but rather greater concern that the political consensus of the global community achieved in 2015 with the SDGs and the climate agreement, could fall apart. It is re-emerging nationalism, populism and short-term political opportunism that are the real threats to sustainability. Europe should have the courage to oppose these threats and stay the course.

Reference

1. *www.ngfs.net: 54 central banks and financial supervisory authorities from all over the world have joined forces in the NGFS to develop concrete measures for a sustainable financial system, not least with a view to the requirements of the structural economic transition triggered by climate change. As of: 12/12/2019.*

Legal Approaches to Encouraging the ECB to Comply with Human Rights Aspects When Establishing the List of Marketable Assets

Marian Szidzek

Abstract This essay deals with the question of whether the European Central Bank may certify reserve adequacy without taking into account compliance with the European Charter of Fundamental Rights by companies whose securities are to be included in the list of marketable assets. It will also be discussed whether there are legal means of enforcing the provisions of the Charter of Fundamental Rights with regard to the European Central Bank's list of marketable assets.

The background to this contribution is the finding of Prof. Bolsinger's study of 13 March 2017 that a large proportion of the securities included in the list of marketable securities are linked to human rights controversies and that little legal attention is paid to this fact. The following description does not claim to be exhaustive, but is rather intended to highlight the problems arising in this context from insufficient consideration of the Charter of Fundamental Rights and the various possibilities for legal enforcement.

1 Legal Background

Pursuant to Article 19 I of the Statute of the ESCB and of the ECB, credit institutions authorised in Member States may be required to hold minimum reserves on accounts with the ECB or the national banks. Pursuant to Art. 19 II of the Statute, the Council, acting in accordance with the procedure laid down in Art. 41, lays down the basis for minimum reserves. The Council made use of this possibility on 11.23.1998 by Council Regulation (EC) No 2531/98, in which it authorised the ECB in Articles 4 and 5 to adopt regulations for the more precise determination and organisation of minimum reserves.

M. Szidzek (✉)
University of Cologne, Köln, Germany

H. Bolsinger et al. (eds.), *The European Central Bank as a Sustainability Role Model*, Sustainable Finance, https://doi.org/10.1007/978-3-030-55450-7_5

The specific requirements to be fulfilled by eligible marketable assets are defined in Guideline (EU) 2015/510 of the ECB.

As collateral, securities of companies may be accepted, inter alia, if they appear on the ECB's list of accepted minimum reserves according to Article 61 I of the Guideline (EU) 2015/510 of the ECB. In this way, the ECB pursues an active economic policy, which is explicitly referred to in Article 282 II Satz 3 TFEU and Article 2 of the Statute of the ESCB and of the ECB, albeit with the words "supportive." The ECB's commitment to the Charter of Fundamental Rights is expressly set out in Art. 51 I GrdRCh. Therefore, the Central Bank as an institution within the meaning of Article 13 I TEU is obliged under Article 51 I GrdRCh in conjunction with Article 6 I TEU not to violate fundamental rights [1].

The objection that this would call into question the independence of the ECB according to Article 282 III TFEU must be firmly countered, "because as a Union institution established by Union law, the ECB, like all Union institutions, is subject to the bindings of Union law and to the control of the Union courts. It can even be said that the ECB's commitment to a clear legal framework is the indispensable counterpart to its far-reaching monetary independence from day-to-day politics." [2] In the view of the ECJ, it is clear that the ECB is required, inter alia, to contribute to the achievement of the objectives set out in Article 2 of the EC Treaty and to fit into the community framework by virtue of the EC Treaty [3].

Due to the diversity of the effects resulting from the obligation to hold minimum reserves and the requirement as to which minimum reserves are accepted, a large number of violations of fundamental rights can be considered. The fact that the financial sector in particular has a special, forward-looking responsibility is impressively demonstrated by the "good governance" concept developed in the 1980s, which established a set of constitutional and institutional requirements for the infrastructure of government and administrative action as a prerequisite for a state to be taken into account when granting loans (e.g. by the World Bank) [4]. The European legislator obviously assumes this itself, as recital 28 of Directive 2013/34/EC of 26 June 2013 shows:

> Since listed companies can play a prominent role in the economies in which they operate, the provisions of this Directive concerning the corporate governance statement should apply to companies whose transferable securities are admitted to trading on a regulated market.

On the one hand, violations of the fundamental rights of natural persons by the companies concerned can be considered.

Here the question arises to what extent private individuals, in contrast to public authorities, are bound to fundamental rights at all, i.e. whether and to what extent an indirect third-party effect of fundamental rights in the sense of an objective value order of the European Charter of Fundamental Rights can be assumed. The possibility of the Charter of Fundamental Rights having an impact on relations between private parties is generally accepted, and in particular any obligations of the Union and the Member States to support private parties, which lead to intervention in private legal relationships, are generally accepted [5].

It follows that the responsibility of the Union institutions, and hence of the ECB, does not end where private law relationships begin. On the contrary, certain types of human rights violations, such as child or forced labour, are typically committed or instigated by companies. It is precisely in such constellations that it is necessary to assume that the Charter of Fundamental Rights and the ECHR are to be taken as a basis for the actions of Union institutions in their relations with and between private individuals, as otherwise they would become completely irrelevant, at least with regard to individual fundamental and human rights.This will be discussed further below.

2 Violations of Fundamental Rights of Natural Persons

A sustainability rating by Prof. Dr. Harald Bolsinger on the minimum reserve securities dated 13 March 2017 showed that the list of accepted securities includes companies that produce weapons of war, practice forced and child labour, are involved in corruption and tax evasion cases and violate environmental regulations.

Accordingly, violations of the scope of protection of Articles 3, 5, 6, 15, III, 24, 27, 28, 31, 32 and 47 of the Charter of Fundamental Rights of the European Union can be considered. In addition, the requirement of Art. 11 TFEU to promote sustainable development is disregarded.

However, the question arises as to the extent to which individual persons concerned can invoke the rights guaranteed in the Charter of Fundamental Rights if they do not possess European citizenship.

The background to this is the fact that within the member states, respect for fundamental and human rights is basically ensured by trade supervisory and criminal law regulations and constitutional control, while the effects of European economic policy do not stop at the borders of the member states.Nevertheless, civil law actions for damages against German companies for human rights violations abroad seem to be the exception rather than the rule for procedural reasons [6].

In principle, third country nationals cannot invoke the fundamental freedoms according to the concept of the fundamental rights protection system, although the ECJ has not yet adopted a position on the question of the fundamental rights ownership of third country nationals.

However, the literature takes the view that third-country nationals should be granted the same protection of fundamental rights if they are affected by Union law in the same way as Union citizens. As an argument for this it is cited that the integration through European law aims precisely at the dismantling of the privileges for its own citizens guaranteed by fundamental rights with regard to economic activities.

In any case, if specific human rights guarantees are in question, a fundamental right of third-country nationals can be assumed. This is supported in particular by the recourse to the ECHR, which does not differentiate between human and civil rights [7].

This is also supported by the fact that the ECHR has also measured violations of fundamental rights by the signatory states to the ECHR on foreign territories against the ECHR standard. It also places an obligation on the member states to ensure that the intergovernmental bodies and international institutions founded by them, including the EU, although not themselves bound by the ECHR, observe the ECHR rights even in concrete individual cases [8].

Accordingly, especially in the case of the above-mentioned serious human rights controversies, it should be possible to affirm the fundamental rights of third country nationals affected by the actions of corresponding companies.

The prohibition of child labour in particular, must be given special consideration and cannot be tied solely to Union citizenship. This is already violated if a person bound by a fundamental right fails to adequately observe the positive obligations resulting from the fundamental right, in particular by failing to enact the provisions necessary to ensure the prohibition of child labour and the necessary protection with regard to working conditions. In addition, they must ensure that the requirements of Article 32 of the EU Charter of Fundamental Rights are enforced in individual cases [9]. Even though the ECB has not been explicitly "burdened" with the enforcement of fundamental rights, it can nevertheless be assumed that it should not be allowed to support child labour by enhancing the value of companies practising it. This is reflected in the fact that, among other things, the awarding of contracts by the Union or the member states to companies involved in forced labour is ruled out, as this is to be understood as direct or indirect promotion of the practices criminalised in Art. 5 GrdRCh [10].

The responsibility of public authorities in general, and thus also of the ECB as a Union institution, which also extends to the effects of economic activity abroad, is also demonstrated by the standards for violations of supervisory and guarantor obligations in relation to criminal offences under Sections 4 and 13 of the International Criminal Code, the allocation of which to business activities seems at least conceivable [11].

This is underlined by the directives modernising EU public procurement law [12], which stipulate that environmental, social and labour law requirements are to be included in the procedures for the award of public contracts by transformation into national law [13].

Finally, the possibility of exceeding competences should be mentioned.

Unlike the member states, the European Union does not have the ability to extend its own competences. To what extent, however, a body other than the European legislator would have the ability of regulating economic policy activities that address a large number of fundamental and human rights issues is highly problematic. However, the obligation to provide minimum reserves and the concrete specification of minimum reserves on the one hand intervenes comprehensively in the private autonomy of credit institutions and on the other hand, the listing of accepted securities certifies the issuing companies a positive status and thus promotes their business conduct.

Whether, with such far-reaching effects of the European Central Bank as a non-legislator, there should be any room for manoeuvre with regard to the extent to which, or even whether, fundamental and human rights violations must be included in the assessment of securities as suitable or not, must be critically questioned. In particular, the principle of monetary independence alone cannot suffice as a justification for this. Whereas the German Federal Constitutional Court, under the terms of parliamentary reservation and the theory of materiality, assumes that fundamental rights issues are to be regulated by the legislature itself [14], corresponding parallels can be drawn in European law within the framework of the prohibition of delegation under Article 290 I TFEU [15]. At this point, the so-called Meroni Doctrine of the European Court of Justice [16] should also be mentioned, which suggests parallels to the BVerfG's theory of materiality [17].

Consequently, it cannot be readily assumed that the ECB has the power to make comprehensive and conclusive rules on minimum reserve requirements, unless the European legislator ensures a sufficient level of protection of fundamental rights outside the borders of the member states, at least with regard to human rights within the meaning of the ECHR, by means of an appropriate framework. If the ECB is not directly responsible for ensuring adequate protection of human rights in the pursuit of its economic policy, the responsibility would have to be sought in the European legislator, which has not sufficiently defined the limits of the ECB's action and has neglected corresponding positive protection obligations.

3 Legal Instruments

In the light of the above, the question arises as to whether there are ways of tackling infringements of fundamental rights through the ECB's reserve eligibility list.

On the one hand, a delimitation must be made as to which system of fundamental rights protection is to be used. On the one hand, legal remedies of the member states, in particular the German constitutional complaint, could be appropriate to take action against violations of fundamental rights through the list of minimum reserves. Legal remedies of the TFEU, in particular the nullity action, could be suitable for this purpose.

Therefore, the relationship between the BVerfG and the European Court of Justice must first be dealt with.

3.1 Prospects of Success of a Nullity Action Pursuant to Art. 263 TFEU

An action for annulment under Art. 263 TFEU against the inclusion of certain securities in the list of marketable assets for the Central Bank could have a chance of success. To do so, it would have to be admissible and justifiable.

The conditions of admissibility of an action for annulment depend on who brings the action. A distinction must be made between the filing by the member states, the European Parliament, the Council or the Commission pursuant to Art. 263 II TFEU, on the one hand, and the so-called privileged right of action, on the other, and the filing by natural or legal persons pursuant to Art. 263 IV, V TFEU. The latter is referred to as an individual invalidity action.

In the first case, the jurisdiction of the ECJ is given under Art. 263 II TFEU, while the CFI has jurisdiction for individual actions for annulment under Art. 256 I TFEU. The active participatory capacity of the Union institutions results from Art. 263 II TFEU, while that of natural and legal persons results from Art. 263 IV, V TFEU. The passive participant capacity of the ECB results from Art. 263 I TFEU.

At this point, it should be noted that, for reasons of clarity, only the chances of success of a nullity action against the ECB itself should be examined in the present case.

However, it would also be conceivable to bring an action against the Council, the Parliament or the Commission if it were assumed that there was insufficient regulatory action on the part of the aforementioned bodies with regard to the list of marketable assets of the Central Bank and that action should be taken against this. In this case, however, an action for failure to act under Art. 265 TFEU would have to be brought.

In the event of an action being brought by the privileged claimants pursuant to Art. 263 I TFEU, the admissible subject-matter of the action shall be legislative acts and acts which are distinct from mere recommendations or opinions. The admissible subject matter of an individual invalidity action, on the other hand, can be acts directly directed against a natural or legal person or legal acts of a regulatory nature which do not entail implementing measures.

First of all, it is questionable which act is to be challenged with the nullity action. It seems obvious to attack the inclusion of securities in the list of marketable assets itself, which should be classified as a resolution on the basis of Article 61 I of the Guideline (EU) 2015/510 of the ECB. This is also legally binding, since no securities can be deposited as collateral that are not included in the list. However, it would also be conceivable to proceed against the basis of authorization enabling this resolution. This would have the advantage of taking action not only retrospectively against the inclusion of individual securities in the list, but also against the general disregard of human rights and sustainability aspects in the core problem laid out in the authorization basis, in order to enforce future compliance with the Charter of Fundamental Rights when securities are included in the list.

However, this question may remain unanswered, since the TFEU is to be understood as a comprehensive system of legal protection [18] and therefore an incident-testing of the basis of authorisation by the European Court of Justice or the European Court of Justice is to be carried out anyway in the case of admissible legal action against the inclusion of individual securities.

Particular difficulties would arise in the context of the standing to bring proceedings. This is generally to be understood as the assertion of individual concern. While the Union institutions, as privileged plaintiffs pursuant to Article 263 II TFEU, do not have to assert the same individual concern on account of their joint responsibility for safeguarding Union law, the plaintiffs of natural and legal persons have to meet high standards. The latter must be either in accordance with Art. 263 IV Alt. 1 TFEU to be affected by an act directly against them, which excludes legislative acts and regulations because of their general-abstract character.

In the present case this would not be the case, since the inclusion of securities in the list of marketable securities is not directed at a person claiming a fundamental right infringement, but concerns the company whose securities are included. However, even this will not be readily understood as the addressee of the resolution, since on the one hand the provisions on the eligibility for minimum reserves concern corresponding credit institutions and on the other hand these are not addressed individually to individual credit institutions, but represent general-abstract provisions which are intended to regulate a number of cases which have not been determined in advance.

Alternatively, however, pursuant to Art. 263 IV Alt. 2 TFEU, action may also be taken against an act which is not directed against the natural person or legal entity but which directly and individually affects it, which also includes general abstract provisions.

According to the second alternative, a decision on the inclusion of securities in the list of marketable securities could be challenged if this directly and individually affects the plaintiff.

For this purpose, the plaintiff would have to be adversely affected by the act challenged [19] and not merely belong to the group of potentially affected persons [20]. In addition, the plaintiff is also individually concerned "if this provision undoubtedly and currently impairs their legal position by restricting their rights or imposing their obligations." [21] However, the decision to take up securities relates first and foremost solely to the discretion of the obligated credit institutions as to which securities they may deposit as collateral with the Central Bank in order to meet the requirements for reserve eligibility. It is true that the decision could be regarded as a measure directly affecting credit institutions in so far as it establishes a binding framework for action on the part of credit institutions and infringements may or must lead to sanctions in order to meet the requirements of the general principle of equal treatment in the form of the principle of self-commitment of the administration.

However, the decision does not create any obligation towards the applicant which would infringe his fundamental rights.

"In view of the fact that monetary policy measures of the ECB regularly require implementing measures and that the Court of First Instance in its previous case-law has not allowed purely factual effects and disadvantages for the individual to suffice for the standing to bring an action, there are hardly any possibilities for non-privileged plaintiffs to successfully bring an action for annulment against such measures."[22] It can therefore be assumed that, in the case of an individual invalidity action, it would at least be dismissed for lack of legal standing if it were based on a direct and individual violation of human rights through the inclusion of securities in the list of marketable securities issued by companies that disregard those human rights.

It could also be considered to bring legal action by legal persons seeking to be affected by the inclusion of such securities in the list of marketable assets in the form of a distortion of competition. This is based on the consideration that the creation of working conditions that comply with the Charter of Fundamental Rights does not initially bring any direct economic benefits, but primarily benefits employees. Although the real value of creating decent working conditions is undeniable, it does not necessarily benefit companies that are committed to this when it comes to assessing creditworthiness in terms of purely mathematical calculations.

This, however, is precisely what the European Central Bank, as an institution of the European Union, should be entitled to do, as it is bound by the Charter of Fundamental Rights, which in turn must be interpreted in the light of the ECHR.

This must apply all the more since Article 29a I of Directive 2014/95/EU requires companies in the public interest to include in their consolidated annual report a consolidated non-financial statement in which information on environmental, social and employee matters, respect for human rights and the fight against corruption and bribery must be provided. The recitals of the Directive set out this point:

3.1.1 Recital 3

> The European Parliament, in its resolutions of 6 February 2013 on corporate social responsibility: accountable, transparent and responsible business practices and sustainable growth' and 'corporate social responsibility' respectively: The European Commission's Communication "Promoting society's interests and a sustainable and inclusive recovery "recognises the importance of disclosure of sustainability information, such as social and environmental factors, by businesses to identify threats to sustainability and strengthen investor and consumer confidence. The provision of non-financial information is an essential element in managing the transition to a sustainable global economy by combining long-term profitability with social justice and environmental protection. [...]

3.1.2 Recital 7

> Where companies are required to make a non-financial statement, the environmental statement should include details of the current and foreseeable environmental and, where appropriate, health and safety impacts of the company's operations, as well as the use of renewable and/or non-renewable energy, greenhouse gas emissions, water consumption and air pollution. With regard to social and workers' concerns, the declaration may include information on measures taken to ensure gender equality, implementation of the basic conventions of the International Labour Organisation, working conditions, social dialogue, respect for the right of workers to be informed and consulted, respect for trade union rights, health and safety at work, dialogue with local communities and/or measures taken to ensure the protection and development of these communities. With regard to human rights and the fight against corruption and bribery, the non-financial declaration could include information on the prevention of human rights violations and/or on existing instruments to combat corruption and bribery.

3.1.3 Recital 10

> Member States should ensure that there are appropriate and effective mechanisms in place to ensure the disclosure of non-financial information by undertakings in accordance with this Directive. To this end, Member States should ensure that effective national procedures are in place to ensure compliance with the obligations laid down in this Directive and that those procedures are open to all natural and legal persons who, under national law, have a legitimate interest in ensuring compliance with the provisions of this Directive.

The declared aim of the European legislator is therefore to ensure that companies in the public interest fulfil their responsibility to prevent human rights violations, combat corruption, promote social justice and protect the environment.

Against this background, however, it seems more than questionable that the Central Bank, as the largest player in the European financial market and at the same time the bearer of official authority directly bound by fundamental rights, does not fulfill this responsibility and that Annex I to Guideline ECB/2011/14 makes no mention of the above-mentioned objectives, or of attempting to contribute to the promotion of decent working conditions and sustainable development in accordance with the CSR Directive.

3.2 Other Possible Courses of Action

The following is a list of other ways in which the Central Bank could be encouraged to take account of the Charter of Fundamental Rights when selecting marketable assets.

First, an action for failure to act pursuant to Art. 265 TFEU could be considered, which is based on the disregard of fundamental rights protection obligations of individuals. However, the question of the right to bring an action also arises here when legal action is brought by natural and legal persons. This is given if the subject of the action is a legal act which, if it had been enacted, could have been the subject of a nullity action, i.e. represents an act with binding legal effects [23]. An omitted act which would have to be regarded as addressed to the applicant is not present if the adoption of a general and normative provision is requested [24]. However, it is precisely the latter that will be assumed with regard to the list of marketable securities, which is why there would be no suitable object of action or the plaintiff's right to bring an action in this case.

A further possibility would be to initiate infringement proceedings pursuant to Art. 259 TFEU, which, however, can only be initiated by the member states and is therefore at the discretion of the these states.

Finally, a constitutional complaint before the Federal Constitutional Court could be considered. This could be based on an identity check, in which it is examined whether Union law and, in carrying it out, also indirectly acts of German violence violate the values laid down in Article 79 III of the Basic Law, in particular respect for human dignity. Similarly, an ultra vires control could be used to check whether secondary Union law exceeds the limits of the competences transferred by the Bundestag within the meaning of Article 23 I sentence 2 of the Basic Law. In the present case, such an overshoot could be seen in the ECB's active economic policy, through rules on minimum reserves and the adoption of marketable assets, which inevitably affects an unmanageable number of persons. According to the principle of parliamentary reservation and the theory of materiality, it must be ensured that fundamental rights issues are regulated by the Bundestag. However, the very fact that the ECB's pursuit of economic policy can result in the promotion of companies linked to human rights controversies was obviously not taken into consideration. The fact that such action is nevertheless possible without a framework to ensure compliance with the Charter of Fundamental Rights could be seen as a violation of the parliamentary reservation and thus as a violation of the limits of the powers conferred by the Bundestag.

However, it should be noted that the BVerfG emphasised in its Honeywell decision that an ultra vires control can only be considered if the conduct of the Union authority contrary to competence is obvious and the challenged act leads to a structurally significant shift in the structure of competences to the detriment of the member states [25].

It follows from the above that it is hardly possible for natural and legal persons to take legal action against the inclusion of securities linked to human rights controversies in the Central Bank's list of marketable assets, even though a fundamental rights obligation of the European Central Bank has been established and it would be necessary to clarify whether it corresponds to this obligation.

It is questionable whether this would sufficiently comply with the rule of law and the requirement of effective legal protection, which is highly doubtful.

If, however, human rights violations by companies are evident and the indirect promotion of them by the Central Bank cannot be legally attacked by individuals and the responsible bodies do not see themselves as being responsible for them either, it becomes clear how important petitions such as the one by Prof. Bolsinger are in making the Central Bank aware of its economic responsibility and its constitutional obligations.

References

1. Angela Schwerdtfeger in: Meyer/Hölscheidt, Charta der Grundrechte der Europäischen Union, 5.2019 edition, GRCh Art. 51 Anwendungsbereich, Rec. 29
2. Selmayr in: von der Groeben/Schwarze/Hatje, Europäisches Unionsrecht, 7. 2015 edition, AEUV Art. 282 [EZB, ESZB und Eurosystem; Zentralbankmandat; Unabhängigkeit; Anhörungsrecht], Rec. 112
3. Judgment of the Court of Justice from July 10th 2003 - Rs. C-11/00; EuR 2003, 864
4. Stelkens in: Stelkens/Bonk/Sachs, Verwaltungsverfahrensgesetz, 9. 2018 edition, Europäisches Verwaltungsrecht, Europäisierung des Verwaltungsrechts und Internationales Verwaltungsrecht, Rec. 254

5. Angela Schwerdtfeger in: Meyer/Hölscheidt, Charta der Grundrechte der Europäischen Union, 5. 2019 edition, GRCh Art. 51 Anwendungsbereich, Rec. 58, 59
6. Kroker, Menschenrechte in der Compliance, CCZ 2015, 120
7. Pieper in: Dauses/Ludwigs, Handbuch des EU-WirtschaftsrechtsWerkstand: 48. EL Juli 2019, B. I. Rechtsquellen, Rec. 154
8. Stelkens in: Stelkens/Bonk/Sachs, Verwaltungsverfahrensgesetz, 9. 2018 edition, Europäisches Verwaltungsrecht, Europäisierung des Verwaltungsrechts und Internationales Verwaltungsrecht, Rec. 256
9. Jarass in: Jarass, Charta der Grundrechte der EU, 3. 2016 edition, EU-Grundrechte-Charta Art.32 Verbot der Kinderarbeit und Schutz der Jugendlichen am Arbeitsplatz, Rec. 11
10. Martin Borowsky in: Meyer/Hölscheidt, Charta der Grundrechte der Europäischen Union, 5. 2019 edition, GRCh Art. 5 Verbot der Sklaverei und der Zwangsarbeit, Rec. 25
11. Kroker, Menschenrechte in der Compliance, CCZ 2015, 126
12. RL 2014/23/EU, RL 2014/24/EU, RL 2014/25/EU
13. Erwägungsgrund 37 der RL 2014/24/EU; Kroker, Menschenrechte in der Compliance, CCZ 2015, 126
14. BVerfG, Decree from 5.9. 1972 - 1 BvR 518/62 u. 308/64, NJW 1972, 1504; BVerfG, Decree from 12.21 1977 - 1 BvL 1/75, NJW 1978, 807;
15. von Danwitz in: Dauses/Ludwigs, Handbuch des EU-Wirtschaftsrechts, Werkstand: 48. EL Juli 2019, B. II. Rechtsetzung und Rechtsangleichung, Rec. 33
16. EuGH, Judgement from 06.13.1958 – 9/56, BeckRS 2004, 73861
17. Gentzsch/Brade: Die Bankenunion vor dem Bundesverfassungsgericht. Neue Impulse für grundlegende Fragestellungen des Verfassungs- und Unionsrechts, EuR 2019, 633
18. EuGH, Judgement from 04.23.1986 – 294/83, BeckRS 2004, 72996
19. Cremer in: Calliess/Ruffert, EUV/AEUV, 5. 2016 edition, AEUV Art. 263 (ex-Art. 230 EGV) [Nichtigkeitsklage], Rec. 35
20. Cremer in: Calliess/Ruffert, EUV/AEUV, 5. 2016 edition, AEUV Art. 263 (ex-Art. 230 EGV) [Nichtigkeitsklage],Rec.36
21. EuG, Rs. T-177/01, Slg. 2002, II-2365, Rec. 51 (Jégo-Quéré/Kommission)
22. Groeben, von der/Schwarze/Anne Schilmöller, 7. 2015edition, Satzung ESZB/EZB Art. 35 Rec. 11
23. Stotz in: Dauses/Ludwigs, Handbuch des EU-Wirtschaftsrechts, Werkstand: 48. EL Juli 2019, P. I. Direkte Klagen, Rec. 233
24. Stotz in: Dauses/Ludwigs, Handbuch des EU-Wirtschaftsrechts, Werkstand: 48. EL Juli 2019, P. I. Direkte Klagen, Rec. 235
25. BVerfGE 126, 286, NJW 2010, 3422

Central Banks in Europe: On the Road to more Sustainability

Susanne Bergius

Abstract The different central banks follow their own different paths to sustainability. The article asks, what types of sustainability they already practice. It describes progressive strategies, looks at the learning processes and analyses the shortcomings. The Network for Greening the Financial System (NGFS) tries to bring all these experiences together and helps the central banks and supervisors contribute to true climate protection and adaptation. But overall, the ecological and social effects of central banks are still underexposed.

Quite a few expectations follow Christine Lagarde's move as the Head of the IMF (International Monetary Fund) to the position as President of the ECB (European Central Bank). Environmentalists expect a more accommodating leadership style regarding sustainability and a more environmentally friendly orientation of future investment policy and perhaps even monetary policy for she believes climate change to be a significant risk, a tangible, financial one, which all banks should be aware of, as she said in September at a hearing in the European Parliament's Economic and Monetary Affairs Committee [1].

Indeed, the ECB can also become active. It manages a pension fund that can safely decide where to invest. However, Lagarde dampened expectations by stating that the ECB can by no means invest its 2.6 trillion euros exclusively in green bonds, for the market for such bonds is much too small for this sum. However, if it sends clear signals that it is increasingly ready and willing to do so in the future, putting more emphasis on such investments, the financial market will take notice. So far, however, very little action has been taken in this direction. Until October 2019, the ECB's website still had a "Climate Change" page. The ECB is a member of the Network for Greening the Financial System (NGFS). It also acquired its first green bonds in 2018.

However in September 2019 it decided to buy 20 billion euros worth of government securities, corporate bonds and covered bonds a month. This program started in November 2019, but it does not draw the line at high fossil fuel consumers or high

S. Bergius (✉)
Journalistin and Moderatorin für Nachhaltiges Wirtschaften und Investieren, Berlin, Germany
e-mail: kontakt@susanne-bergius.de

H. Bolsinger et al. (eds.), *The European Central Bank as a Sustainability Role Model*, Sustainable Finance, https://doi.org/10.1007/978-3-030-55450-7_6

emissions issuers. This means that the ECB has fallen far behind many a European central bank.

What types of sustainability are progressive central banks in Europe already practicing? This will be explained by the following questions:

1. What impact can central banks achieve—or avoid?
2. What are progressive central banks in Europe doing in concrete terms?
3. How consistent are the central banks at the forefront of sustainability?
4. What do these pioneers really achieve in the world of central banking?
5. What is the Network for Greening the Financial System (NGFS) doing?
6. Does this trend really cover the thematic breadth of sustainability?

1 What Impact Can Central Banks Achieve—Or Avoid?

At the end of 2018, Bundesbank board member Joachim Würmeling said that one should not overestimate the impact of central banks' investment portfolios. Indeed, the scale of their investments is merely a drop in the bucket in the hundred-trillion-dollar-capital market. The world's leading central banks have in total an estimated $20 trillion in assets [2].

Nevertheless, they can still send important signals to the financial market. Their decisions and their actions are observed closely, and this does not only pertain to the prime rate. After all, the members of the NGFS central bank network make up "three-quarters of the world's systemically vital banks and two-thirds of the word's systemically vital insurers", as Bundesbank Executive Board member Sabine Mauderer stated in an article in the *Süddeutsche Zeitung* in July 2019 [3]. Therefore central banks can foster a more sustainable financial system and more sustainable economic development—or they can curb this development. A choice must be made.

According to Philip Lane, at the time the Governor of the Central Bank of Ireland, his bank is "… well placed to take a system-wide and holistic perspective on the implications of climate change for the financial system." [4] This is particularly true when, like the Irish and Dutch, they act as both regulatory and supervisory bodies.

"The distributive effect of what central banks do is immense," says Alexander Barkawi, founder and director of the Council on Economic Policies (CEP) in Zurich [5]. This is all the more true as they have massively expanded their capital market activities since the financial crisis of 2008. What is needed now is an in-depth analysis of the extent to which purchases of government and corporate bonds and, depending on the country, even equities counteract sustainability goals.

A study by the Grantham Research Institute in 2017 revealed that this is indeed the case. According to the study, the ECB and the Bank of England appear to be relatively heavily invested in emissions-heavy sectors through the purchases of corporate bonds. According to the authors, this is an imbalance. Sini Matikainen, one of the study's authors, states: "However, even supposedly market-neutral interventions by central banks may show an unintended structural bias towards carbon-intensive industry incumbents." This may lead to price distortion and stimulate companies with high CO2 emissions to take on more debt. Therefore, "Central banks should investigate the impact of their interventions on both high-carbon and low-carbon investment." [6]

According to Barkawi, the fact that the ECB has begun buying securitizations of automobile loans in its Asset-Backed-Securities-Purchase-Program as of fall 2014 is "another example of support of individual sectors that should be reviewed." The ECB states that it must stay neutral, "but it is not", Barkawi replied. By deciding to buy car loans, it has established distortions in favor of a particular sector. "Companies which are heavily indebted within the market benefit more than average from the purchase of corporate bonds. Companies that don't issue bonds at all are completely left out." [7]

The Österreichische Nationalbank, the central bank of Austria, implicitly confirmed the before mentioned negative effects in an invitation for an international conference on "Green finance, regulation and monetary policy" in 2018, where it and the other organizers wrote: "Monetary policy activities of central banks may unintentionally favor environmentally harmful activities." [8] They referred to empirical studies which supported this idea, and also pointed to possibilities of rectifying this behavior. Clearly, the alleged neutrality is a misconception.

Alexander Barkawi believes that price stability is the ECB's primary, but not its only task, "supporting the general economic policies and objectives of the European Union—and thus also the objective of sustainability—is explicitly part of its mandate by law."

Central banks must, therefore, also concern themselves with sustainability. This much was also stated by the former head of the ECB, Mario Draghi in September 2017. Draghi, who held the position until the end of October 2019, told the Committee on Monetary and Economic Affairs of the European Parliament that the mandate of the ECB does indeed include secondary objectives in addition to the primary objective of price stability. One of his secondary objectives included the sustainable development of Europe and the improvement of the quality of the environment [9].

A healthy environment is a fundamental human right and is established by law in the Charter of Fundamental Rights of the European Union. Although the ECB is not explicitly bound by this, the Charter applies to all EU institutions under the Treaty of Lisbon.

2 What Are Progressive Central Banks in Europe Doing in Concrete Terms?

They are cultivating different fields in different ways. Four perfect examples of banks that are behaving in this manner are: De Nederlandsche Bank (DNB), the Banque de France, the Norwegian Norges Bank and the Swedish Rijksbank.

Before taking a look at each individual bank within this context it is important to note that the term "sustainable finance" is spreading within the financial world. However, some are spearheading a "sustainable financial system" or a "more sustainable" one, while others interpret it as simply more sustainable financing or merely "green" financing—without making any large structural changes. How central banks and policymakers interpret the term is a good indicator for understanding their activities.

2.1 *De Nederlandsche Bank (DNB)*

In mid-March 2019, the central bank of the Netherlands DNB became the first in the world to sign the UN Principles for Responsible Investment PRI [10] and to draft a "Responsible Investment Charter." [11] It aims to "make the economy more sustainable and manage the ESG risks of its own reserves." It also proposes to invest 19 billion euros responsibly. ESG stands for "environment,—social—governance".

By signing the six principles [12], the DNB has not only committed itself to taking ESG risks and opportunities into account in investment decisions and portfolio management, but it has also committed itself to engaging in direct dialogue with risky issuers. This will be done either on a one on one basis or with other major investors as support. The purpose is to aid the issuers in conducting their business in a more environmentally and socially responsible manner. Last but not least, the bank must meet annual progress milestones which must be made public. The PRI has been endorsed by the banks pension funds already in 2011, so the bank is aware of the procedure.

DNB, which is also a supervisory body, hopes to "inspire other central banks as well as the financial sector" by sharing information regarding its approach. The strategy, set to be implemented by 2025, aims to promote two things: "sustainable economic growth that does not harm the environment" and an "inclusive financial and economic system". "We want to practice what we preach", Executive Director Frank Elderson told US Senators in Washington D.C. in October 2019 [13].

Thereby the Dutch are strengthening their role as pioneers among the central banks. The DNB is very active and has been positioning itself in this role for quite a while. In 2017 DNB President Klaas Knot substantiated this as follows: "Not taking relevant long-term risks and long-term prosperity into account, would be contrary to our mandate." [14] Prosperity that causes great ecological damage or burdens the social cohesion of a society would not be sustainable in the long term, he stated.

The DNB therefore conducted intensive research into sustainability. Since 2016, it has been analyzing the climate and transition risks for the national economy and since 2017 it has been using stress tests to assess the climate risks for financial institutions, pension funds and the financial system as a whole; the flat Netherlands are particularly threatened by a rise in sea level. According to an exploration of climate-related risks focusing on sea water level increases [15], conducted by the DNB, costs and loan defaults would be high.

This is why De Nederlandsche Bank (DNB) established a platform for sustainable financing [16] in 2016 and why it is involved in the Dutch Climate Agreement of 2018 [17]. In 2019, nearly the entire Dutch financial sector started to implement methods to measure the carbon footprint of its investments and loans. These are to be made public as of 2020. And by 2022 at the latest, the institutions want to set themselves reduction targets and report on their progress.

Because banks, insurers and pension funds have not yet given sufficient consideration to climate risks, as their 2017 analysis [18] proved, the DNB is now integrating the factor of climate risks into its supervision so that financial institutions not only identify the risks, but also ensure that they manage them, as Elderson explained in October 2019. The DNB announced to publish a good practice guide for banks and insurance companies to accelerate a movement in this direction.

There will also be a fact sheet on new ESG regulations for pension providers. This means that DNB does not draw the line at simply climate issues. But it also identifies risks with regard to the UN Sustainable Development Goals, the SGDs. In May 2019, its study "Values at Risk?" [19] found that the Dutch financial sector may face problems such as water scarcity, raw material scarcity, biodiversity loss and human rights controversies. Elderson commented on this by stating: "It is therefore only natural and clearly within our mandate to continue to broaden our joint work in these areas." [20] The analysis of 25 financial institutes showed, "that most have not yet fully integrated their sustainability efforts into their operational management". In addition, the government called for more adequate pricing of CO2 emissions and a climate law as stronger incentives for sustainable investment to slow down climate change and achieve the Paris Accord climate goals [21].

In its 2018 annual report [22], the Institute intends to point out further regulatory necessities where appropriate. It presents CSR goals, measures, activities and achievements in an exemplary overview—others should take this as an example [23].

2.2 *Banque de France*

A look at the French central bank illustrates the enormous discrepancy in thinking and acting between the different monetary watchdogs. It is miles ahead of its contemporaries. Ivan Odonnat, Deputy General Director Financial Stability and

Operations, made this clear. While most financial actors and central banks favor a voluntary approach, he stated in automn 2018: "We are in favour of moving from a voluntary to a mandatory approach." [24] This could be a comply-or-explain rule, whereby actors must meet certain requirements and if not explain why they are not able to. Odonnat continued with: "In other words, the NGFS members are first in line."

NGFS stands for "Network for Greening the Financial System." This network was initiated by the Swedish Financial Supervisory Authority (Finansinspektionen) out of concern regarding climate change, recognizing that central banks are being called upon to take this risk into account. They were met with an open ear in Paris. Consequently, they and the Banque de France established the "NGFS" in 2017. Odonnat stated that the reason being, "in the face of climate change, we need to go much further than we have done so far" and do so in a structured way. More incentives would be needed for both the public and private sectors.

This does not only apply to climate aspects. Therefore the Banque de France adopted a "Responsible Investment Charter" [25] as early as March 2018 and has since been one of the first central banks to pursue so-called "ESG integration" implementing the systematic observance of key environmental, social and organizational management criteria in its own funds in order to invest responsibly. "This is in line with our fiduciary responsibility and is a contribution to financial stability," says Odonnat. A previous analysis revealed that 14 percent of the risks within the portfolios were related to industry transformation: the necessary transition to a low-emission, environmentally and socially responsible economy. Their portfolios should contribute to this transformation. The institute wants to make best practice examples transparent.

At the end of 2018 Odonnat also announced that the Banque de France would start reporting on climate risks in line with the recommendations of the Financial Stability Board's Task Force on Climate-Related Financial Disclosures (TCFD) [26]. At that time, it had just started tackling the challenge, beginning with a portfolio of responsible investments.

At the same event, Würmeling from the Bundesbank sounded off a completely differing view point. He said that the disclosure recommended by the TCFD was intended to be transparent for investors and, "since no-one invests in central banks, TCFD disclosures are irrelevant." He probably views this differently today for the Banque de France is the first central bank to publish a report on its "responsible investment" [27], which is explicitly based on the TCFD recommendations. Moreover, part of the activities of the central bank network, of which the Bundesbank is a member, is based on the work of the TCFD.

2.3 *Norges Bank*

Norway's central bank is also among the leaders. Its investment department is responsible for the capital investments of Norway's one trillion dollar sovereign wealth fund. The fund has been heeding environmental and social criteria since 2004 and has an ethics committee. The asset management department must comply with its decisions and sell securities which are deemed to be highly critical after careful examination and dialogue with the issuers. The powerful pension fund was the first major investor worldwide to publicly announce that it was selling companies or excluding them from its investments due to ethical reasons.

As a result, the central bank of Norway has been dealing with sustainability aspects, including human rights and working conditions, for much longer than other banks. The Norges Bank Investment Management (NBIM) co-founded the PRI in 2006. Since 2012, it has sold a total of 240 companies and excluded certain sectors from its investment portfolio altogether: tobacco, palm oil, cement, oil sands, coal-based power generation and as of 2016, the coal industry [28]. At the same time, it has established extensive environmental investment mandates, equity participation and green bonds, over 60 billion kroner by the end of 2018. The bank also analyses corporate activities that lead to deforestation which in turn results in increases emissions as part of its focus on climate change. In fact it is one of the first major investors to take deforestation into consideration.

In 2018 it also raised its expectations regarding the banking sector, demanding more information on the financing of fossil fuels and renewable energies in order to be able to assess the extent to which banks are exposed to risks in the transition to a low-carbon emitting economy.

This is a clear implementation of a TCFD recommendation. In its 2018 annual report it also explains in accordance with these recommendations how it calculates the climate-damaging emissions of its share and bond portfolio. This puts it well ahead of other central banks. Moreover, the NBIM released a statement [29] that detailed how investors like themselves can contribute to the UN sustainability goals, the SDGs: by providing capital to companies and exercising their ownership rights, i.e. by conducting active dialogues in favor of greater sustainability [30]. As a driving force of sustainability it is also seeking more governmental support regarding other investment opportunities and a greater degree of freedom regarding more sustainable strategies. However, this is not always met with success.

2.4 *Riksbank*

The Riksbank, Sweden's central bank, sold government bonds issued by foreign states citing climate change reasons. According to analysts, it is the first central bank in the world to do so. Deputy Governor Martin Flodén justified the move in a speech in November 2019: "The Riksbank needs to analyze and manage the economic consequences of climate change. Although it is the government and the Riksdag who should formulate climate policy, we can contribute to the climate work to some extent by giving consideration to sustainability aspects when investing in the foreign exchange reserves. We are now doing this by rejecting issuers who have a large climate footprint." [31]

This is why bonds issued by the Canadian province of Alberta and the Australian states of Queensland and Western Australia were sold in 2019. In 2018 already the Board of Directors of Sweden's central bank decided to consider sustainability aspects in all investment decisions.

3 How Consistent Are the Central Banks at the Forefront of Sustainability?

Reaching sustainability is a process of learning and change, but sometimes there is a lack of stringency. This can be seen in several cases in Norway, the Netherlands, Germany and Switzerland.

3.1 Case in Point: De Nederlandsche Bank

This bank carries out climate stress tests for financial institutions. However, it has not yet analyzed its own portfolio—at least there is no evidence of this in the 2018 annual report. This should change with PRI membership, which requires the integration of ESG aspects into the investment practices of its own reserves and an annual progress report—including climate effects. Frank Elderson the Executive Director of the DNB stated, "One of the main challenges we are currently facing in this process is the lack of data needed to actually quantify climate risk."

The DNB must overcome this hurdle. He continued: "We have learned that a lack of climate-related financial regulation does not prevent us from acting now. Because we are mandated to supervise all relevant risks, we did not need additional legislation or regulations to start acting on these risks today." [32]

But at the end of 2017 central bank president Knot was quite defensive regarding the question whether central banks should use their monetary policy to stimulate green investments or to discourage fossil investments. In general, he said, central banks are quite cautious about using their central implementation instruments for goals other than inflation and financial stability. "However we are aware of the enormous challenge of stopping global warming, and its potentially devastating consequences if we don't do enough. That's why we think it's vital to ask ourselves whether central banks and financial regulators should play a more active role in facilitating green financing." [33] According to members of the audience, he ended his speech by saying: "Let us consider everything with an open mind."

3.2 Case in Point: German Bundesbank

In the past the Bundesbank was certainly not a pioneer with regard to sustainability issues. In the meantime, however, it has become concerned with these issues. Since 2007 it has been aiding public institutions to take ESG criteria into account in their provisions for civil servants' pensions as their asset manager. But such criteria were rare for a long time and have by no means become the norm. In autumn 2019 board member Mauderer told the press that 10 out of 16 clients display great interest. Though, expectations are often very different. Meanwhile, the Bundesbank, as the asset manager of the federal and state governments, has invested for them a higher seven-figure sum under sustainability criteria.

The roles are clearly defined in this third-party portfolio: the customers' task is to define sustainability criteria, while the Bundesbank is responsible for the operational implementation of investment decisions. This was the situation for a long time.

Now, this has changed. On October 29, 2019 the Bundesbank held its second financial markets conference with the overlying theme: "Sustainable Finance—a Game Changer for our Financial System?" On the other hand, in its October report [34], it criticized vague guidelines and a lack of transparency in sustainable investments and called for clearer guidelines.

Nevertheless, under the pressure of public opinion, it has taken action. Speaking at the second financial markets conference in Frankfurt, executive board member Mauderer said: "We at the Bundesbank are currently reviewing how sustainable our own euro portfolio is and where there is still potential for development." Days before, she told the press more concrete that the institute was in the process of defining criteria for its own investments of over twelve billion euros. Prior to this statement she had written a guest article for the *Süddeutsche Zeitung* in July saying: "All central banks are called upon to set a good example and to orient their own portfolio management towards sustainability." [35]

It will be interesting to see whether the Deutsche Bundesbank will sort out securities for environmental and social reasons and report on them as transparently as the Norwegians.

Commenting on the title of the conference "Sustainable Finance" Mauderer explained that sustainability is such a "game changer", "something that changes everything—changes the way we think and how we act." [36] However, both Mauderer and the head of the Bundesbank, Jens Weidmann, want to curb the expectations toward their institute [37]. Monetary policy should not be too encumbered by environmental policy goals. Mauderer stressed that "Climate risks entail considerable financial risks and are therefore a very important issue for central banks. However, central banks cannot be our 'climate fire fighters'".

They believe that it is more difficult to integrate sustainability into their "Politik-Portfolio". Regarding the ECB's monetary policy of currency reserves and bond purchases the Bundesbank also invests in green bonds; though, this is less than one percent.

Mauderer repeatedly emphasizes that the Bundesbank acts in a market-neutral manner and does not directly intend to trigger positive ecological or social impulses with its investments, but rather to reduce financial climate risks. In this respect, the Frankfurt institution differs greatly from other leaders who, like the DNB and Banque des France, are clearly committed to climate protection and sustainable development in line with the UN Sustainable Development Goals.

3.3 *Case in Point: The Swiss National Bank*

The Swiss National Bank (SNB) considers itself to be an investor who bears co-responsibility for its portfolio investments. Since the end of 2013, its investment policy guidelines have included the following requirement: "The SNB also avoids shares in companies which produce internationally banned weapons, seriously violate fundamental human rights or systematically cause severe environmental damage." [38] With this clause it pulled far ahead of other central banks.

However, WWF Switzerland's Senior Advisor of Sustainable Finance at that time, Ivo Mugglin, said to me that the environmental organization considers this to be a "very vague statement". For it is unclear how it actually incorporates sustainability into its investment decisions. According to the media, there has not been much exclusion.

In addition, the SNB does not examine how climate risks could affect the stability of the Swiss financial market. It is not even clear whether the bank even classifies climate related damage as "systematically severe environmental damage".

In contrast to that, Andréa Maechler, member of the SNB Governing Board, gave a statement to the press which publicly objected to the idea that the bank was ignoring climate issues. She reiterated that the exclusion criteria also take climate issues into account and that they are implemented very professionally and in a very structured manner across the entire investment portfolio [39].

On the other hand, in February the *Luzerner Zeitung* declared, on the basis of data from the US Securities and Exchange Commission (SEC), that the SNB had purchased US fossil fuel stocks [40]. At the end of 2019 the NGO "Artisans de la Transition" criticized the SNB for being responsible for the emission of as much greenhouse gas as Switzerland emits in an entire year. This, it stated, is due to the fact that the SNB invests 10.8% of its US stock portfolio in fossil fuel industry based companies, according to a study published in December 2016: "The Swiss National Bank's US financial investments in fossil fuel industry companies: a disaster for return and climate." [41]

The Climate Alliance Switzerland claims that the SNB's equity investments are responsible for more than Switzerland's annual CO2 emissions and that they are promoting a temperature rise of 4–6 degrees. The Alliance brings together key representatives from the areas of education, science, business, civil society, the financial world and politics. In 2017, the Climate Alliance contradicted the bank's argument climate-friendly investments would oppose its legal mandate, in an open letter to the SNB Governing Board. It called on it to identify and publish the emissions of its global portfolio and to develop an exit scenario for the largest emitters.

In April 2018, the Climate Alliance sent recommendations [42] regarding climate risks to the SNB. Consequently, climate sensitive investments are not only compatible with the bank's mandate for financial stability, but are an integral part of it.

One year later, in April 2019, the SNB joined the network of central banks. Regarding the reasons for this action it simply states: "The SNB's goal in joining the NGFS is to engage in dialogue and share knowledge in order to better understand and anticipate the potential impact of climate risks on macroeconomics and financial stability." [43]

However, it has not yet adapted its 2015 revised investment guidelines in this regard. It also does not provide any information online about possible climate risk research it may conduct. Time will tell what actions it will take in the future.

3.4 Case in Point: Norges Bank

In the past the bank recommended that the pension fund should be opened up to unlisted infrastructure investments. However, according to the Institute for Energy Economics and Financial Analysis (IEEFA) the Ministry of Finance rejected this proposal. In a 2017 report [44], the IEEFA's Director of Finance, Tom Sanzillo, urged that Norway's sovereign wealth fund should benefit, like others have, from the massive investment potential of renewable energies.

In November 2017, the Norges Bank also proposed to the Norwegian Minister of Finance, Siv Jensen, that the Norwegian wealth fund should no longer invest in oil and gas companies. It made the move together with the pension funds which is under its supervision. "This was a remarkable step," said Joseph Zacune of the European Climate Foundation [45]. After all, the pension fund is fed by the country's large oil revenues, and this is also why the central bank knows that they are finite and that investing in them is risky.

The Minister of Finance was reported to have been quite astonished. In February 2018, she formed a group of experts to shed light on the 4% of energy investments [46]. It recommended to continue investing in the energy-intensive shares and to reduce risks in some other way. Their recommendations were put up for public discussion in September 2018 [47]. The government wanted to make a decision in the first half of 2019, but till mid of November nothing has officially been decided yet.

In any case, according to the 2018 annual report, the NBIM did not systematically get out of oil stocks. It analyzed a number of the companies in its portfolio who were said to have much higher emission rates than others in the same sector—and sold shares of only one unnamed company [48].

For the environmental activists in "Extinction Rebellion" this is not enough. At the end of May 2019 they blocked the entrance of the Norwegian central bank to protest the wealth fund's continued investment in companies that burn coal.

According to the German daily FAZ they accused the pension fund managed by the central bank of taking insufficient measures in the fight against climate change.

The examples from Switzerland and Norway clearly illustrate that central banks should no longer operate independently of society; instead it quickly becomes apparent when they do not act, or are not allowed to act.

4 What Do These Pioneers Really Achieve in the World of Central Banking?

In the last three years a change in attitude can be observed. Both the pioneers and civil society have contributed to this, as the Swiss example/case in point shows.

This rising awareness was encouraged principally by Mark Carney, the long-standing Governor of the Bank of England (BoE), who caused quite a stir with his demands and proclamations that institutional investors should consider climate, environmental, social and governmental aspects.

Meanwhile, central banks worldwide are increasingly becoming concerned with sustainability. This can be seen through their advocacy, motivation, supervisory activities and increasingly with regard to their own investments. At the very least they are addressing the risks of global warming, as can be seen in the DNB in 2017, the Bundesbank in 2018 and the Central Bank of Ireland 2019. They call on commercial banks to consider climate change in their risk management.

In early February 2019, Philip Lane, then Governor of the Central Bank of Ireland and now the ECB's new Chief Economist, announced that climate risks were systemic and a strategic priority in his central bank's task of ensuring monetary and financial stability. According to Lane, stability risks are particularly likely to arise if the transition to low-CO2 technologies is too slow, which would require stronger interventions with higher risks: "climate resilience is an integral component of the overall resilience of the financial system and the economy." [49]

Faced with these threats, eight central banks and supervisory authorities established the Network for Greening the Financial System (NGFS) in December 2017 [50]. Their aim is to "make the financial system greener" by sharing experiences and identifying best practices. This sent a clear signal to the rest of the central bank community.

The central banks in Paris and Stockholm wisely integrated the Bundesbank which was hesitant at the time. It became a founding member, although it had reacted very defensively when confronted with its role in the face of climate change earlier that year.

At an NGFS event in Berlin in November 2018 board member Joachim Würmeling admitted that their position had changed: "We have put a lot of thought into it, analyzed it, have become aware of the risks and are now able to see some options of what central banks can do." He admitted: "It's naive not to act."

While central banks should continue to pursue the objective of price stability in a market-neutral manner, they should also support the transition to a more sustainable economy. This is now one of Sabine Mauderer's main tasks while serving on the Bundesbank's Executive Board and in the NGFS.

The progressive players have rapidly developed this network of central banks and supervisory authorities into a global platform. Its activities are widely recognized and more and more institutions are joining. It has become nearly impossible for central banks to circumvent.

The pioneers also have influence on the ECB, as they sit on their Executive Board. This was made clear by Frenchman Benoit Coeuré, who has been a member of the Executive Board for eight years. In November 2018 in Berlin, he emphasized that all authorities, including the ECB, must consider how to appropriately react to climate change. It poses a fundamental risk for banks. "Climate change can be expected to affect monetary policy one way or the other." [51] This could be substantial. Climate change may make it more difficult to correctly identify crises. This identification is important in discerning medium-term inflation forecasts. Extreme events may limit the political latitude of central banks and force them to make alternative decisions.

5 What Is the Network for Greening the Financial System (NGFS) Doing?

More and more central banks and supervisory authorities are joining this group—there are already 66 members (August 2020)—nearly all the top players are members with the notable exception of the American Fed. Currently, the network intends to bring more central banks in developing countries on board, as the poorest regions of the world are most affected by the consequences of climate change.

The NGFS is committed to helping to achieve the Paris climate goals. Secondly, it aims to strengthen the role of the financial system to manage risks and to mobilize capital for green and low-carbon-emission investments in favor of environmentally sustainable development. These are purely voluntary initiatives. Proposals for binding political guidelines have not been planned. Instead, the institutes are working on reports and methods to better assess climate risks.

The first NGFS progress report was published in mid-October 2018 [52]. It describes the limits of climate risk assessments in a rather defensive manner. These limits are due in large part to the quality and availability of data and a lack of understanding of the financial risk differences between "green" and "brown" (emission-heavy) investments. Therefore, the report calls for the development of new analytical and supervisory approaches, including those involving future scenario analysis and stress testing.

In April 2019, the NGSF published another report entitled "A Call for Action—Climate Change as a Source of Financial Risk." [53] It describes how various climate and environmental risks affect the financial markets. It called on central banks and supervisory authorities to adopt best practices in four key areas. These include taking greater consideration of climate risks in financial reporting and in the assessment of financial stability.

In mid-October 2019, the network published "A Sustainable and Responsible Investment Guide for Central Banks' Portfolio Management at the IMF Annual Meetings." [54] It is intended to encourage central banks to consider sustainability aspects in their various portfolios—be it through exclusionary criteria regarding the purchasing of corporate shares and bonds, be it through active dialogues with issuers or be it through the impact-oriented purchase of green bonds.

A survey conducted for this first global assessment revealed that 25 of the 27 responding central banks said that they have adopted SRI criteria in their own investment portfolios or plan to do so. This sounds like more than it is. It applies to 53 percent of the bank's own portfolios. However, the high percentages are explained by the fact that only member central banks were surveyed. Non-member central banks were not. In their case, the percentages are likely to be very low, even near zero. This also applies to the other types of portfolios, where the rates of the respondents range from 25 to 46 percent. It is also unclear how comprehensive the policies truly are.

Seven central banks from Norway, Italy, France, Hungary, Switzerland, the Netherlands and Mexico explain how they developed a sustainable or responsible investment strategy in the 2019 Investment Guide. "Sustainable and responsible investment is increasingly driving central banks," says Mauderer. The guide was developed under her direction which makes it all the more surprising that the Bundesbank failed to set an example. This proves that it does not yet belong among the leaders of the financial world.

6 Does This Trend Really Cover the Thematic Breadth of Sustainability?

A crucial issue concerning the NGFS is that although this network seems to inherently stand for a "greener" future, the term "greening" is a part of its name, and that it clearly focuses on climate issues, as does the ECB [55], other highly relevant environmental issues are not addressed.

Some of the inherent issues which the NGFS does not address are: the dramatic increase in the species extinction rate [56], which threatens our very existence, and social living conditions, the improvement of which is indispensable from a human rights and labor rights perspective.

The Banque de France and De Nederlandsche Bank are well ahead of the other central banks due to their holistic sustainability strategies.

The relevance of this issue is demonstrated by the amount of problematic securities in the ECB's portfolio, as reported in the German *Handelsblatt Business Briefing*

Sustainable Investment in April 2018 [57]. According to a 2017 study by the Grantham Research Institute [58], the ECB appears to have invested relatively heavily in emissions-heavy sectors via the purchase of corporate bonds.

In addition, according to analyses by various rating agencies, the ECB has been undermining fundamental EU values relating to human rights and environmental protection with part of its investments for some years. A petition [59] has been circulating in the EU Parliament since 2017 to protest this action; the Committee on Petitions is dealing with this issue. The portfolio's emission levels contradict its 2017 statement that it supports the EU Commission action plan on sustainable finance and that it "supports the flow of capital into sustainable sectors." [60]

Some stakeholders are calling for the EU to impose investment requirements requiring the ECB and central banks to respect environmental, social and governance issues. However it is highly unlikely that the EU will implement such measures. Its 2018 Commission action plan on financing sustainable growth [61] does not stipulate such actions. Nor is the new elected commission likely to address the systemic role of central banks. Firstly, the job descriptions of the new EU Commission President Ursula von der Leyen for the key commissioners lack the EU Action Plan Sustainable Finance; secondly, the commission has defined sustainable finance to mean only "green finance" and above all to simply mean climate-friendly investments [62].

The focus on climate change is also reflected in the International Platform on Sustainable Finance [63] established by the European Commission at the IMF Annual Meeting in October 2019. Despite the claim to "sustainability" carried in its name, its goal is to mobilize international private funds towards green and climate-friendly investments. Its members include central banks, and the NGFS is an observer. By reducing sustainability to mere climate protection and climate adaptation, the EU Commission fails to recognize the power of the financial market guardians.

In 2018 the ECB purchased 30 billion euros in bonds per month, and Alexander Barkawi of the Council on Economic Policies (CEP) in Zurich criticized that "there is no comprehensive discussion regarding the extent to which environmental and social risks are reflected in this policy." [64] Since September 2019, as the ECB announced to revive its monthly bond purchase program which will entail 20 billion euros a month, there is, with the exception of individual critics and the meeting of the Weltethos Institut on October 29, 2019, just as little political and social discourse regarding this issue as there was in the past.

In October 2019, the German Council for Sustainable Development (RNE) took up the issue and, in a "Statement on the Sustainable Finance Strategy," [65] called on the German government to "hold the European Central Bank (ECB) accountable regarding the principle of sustainability." In some instances the statement may appear somewhat contradictory. However it is very clear in saying that it is a "certainty that securities linked to corruption, environmental destruction, human rights violations and the production of banned weapons are in direct contradiction to the required financial security and that the purchasing of such assets must be stopped immediately."

In other words, the ecological and social effects of central bank activities are still underexposed.

At the same time however, Norway's central bank clearly indicated the limits of capital investment in this regard. Norges Bank Investment Management (NBIM) protested in a public letter [66] to the PRI that the signatories could not have voted on a chapter in the PRI's 10-year plan that deals with the impact of investors on the UN's sustainability goals, i.e. the Sustainable Development Goals (SDGs). The "Blueprint for Responsible Investment" [67] describes nine activities through which the PRI seeks to support its members, including "enabling real world impact aligned with the SDGs."

The NBIM argues that this impact orientation is a "fundamental strategic development" and "de facto a new principle" that comes on top of the existing six PRI principles. The expanded orientation could be interpreted as the "expectation that financial investors should have dual or multiple objectives." The NBIM voiced their reservations regarding this new measure during the consultations on the PRI Blueprint in 2017 and again in April 2019 during the consultation [68] on the revised framework for annual reporting by PRI members. It warned the organization that "including outcome-based reporting in the PRI Reporting Framework is drifting away from the PRI's founding principles."

The mega-investor makes several objective arguments against outcome-based reporting related to the SDGs. Firstly, the political objectives do not always have investable characteristics. Secondly, investors would need to prove an additional impact of their investments which would be impossible for smaller investors to do for they have no real influence on the companies. Thirdly, the complex interactions within the 17 goals make measuring the impact challenging, especially because normative judgements are called for. Lastly, investors cannot be expected to provide outcome-based reporting unless eco-social and/or political goals are directly mandated by their shareholders.

The financial world and the academic community must take a serious look at these arguments and discuss whether there are possible solutions to these dilemmas.

6.1 Outlook

In the future, it will be vital to keep a close eye on what the ECB and other central banks contribute toward "sustainable finance": and here I mean a sustainable financial system that enables sustainable economic development—I don't say: growth—and a sustainable society in accordance with the SDGs.

It will also be of interest to see if some of the banks respond to a proposal made by the think tank WAAS. The "World Academy of Art and Science" was founded by Albert Einstein and proposes a parallel digital currency in order to specifically finance global common goods and at the same time stabilize the existing currency system. A central bank mandate for a virtual currency earmarked for SDG projects could hypothetically, thanks to new liquidity, end poverty within one year and stabilize consumer prices as well as democratic systems within two years and last but not least create millions of new jobs.

According to WAAS member Professor Stefan Brunnhuber, various field trials in different regions and on various aspects of digital currencies have already demonstrated the immense potential of this idea [69]. The idea is centered on a Euro-convertible system, with the European Central Bank or governments the issuers of the digital currency.

Since 2019 WAAS experts are engaged in "constructive discussions" with the UN, the World Bank, regulators and central banks both nationally and internationally. It will be interesting to see what the outcome of these talks will be.

References

1. Björn Finke: Lagarde im Kreuzverhör, Süddeutsche Zeitung, Sept. 5, 2019.
2. https://www.handelsblatt.com/downloads/21167578/6/hb-buisiness-briefing-investments_04_18.pdf
3. Sylvie Goulard & Sabine Mauderer: „Mit gutem Beispiel vorangehen", in: Süddeutsche Zeitung, 7.8.2019
4. https://www.centralbank.ie/docs/default-source/publications/economic-letters/vol-2019-no-1-climate-change-and-the-irish-financial-system-(lane).pdf?sfvrsn=8
5. https://www.handelsblatt.com/downloads/21167578/6/hb-buisiness-briefing-investments_04_18.pdf
6. http://www.lse.ac.uk/GranthamInstitute/publication/the-climate-impact-of-quantitative-easing/
7. https://www.handelsblatt.com/downloads/21167578/6/hb-buisiness-briefing-investments_04_18.pdf
8. https://www.suerf.org/greenfinance2018 (Accessed 11.05.2019)
9. http://www.europarl.europa.eu/cmsdata/128520/Monetary_dialogue_25092017EN.pdf,
10. https://www.dnb.nl/en/news/news-and-archive/Persberichten2019/dnb382879.jsp
11. https://www.dnb.nl/en/binaries/DNB%20Responsible%20Investment%20Charter_tcm47-382883.pdf
12. https://www.unpri.org/pri/an-introduction-to-responsible-investment/what-are-the-principles-for-responsible-investment
13. https://www.dnb.nl/nieuws/nieuwsoverzicht-en-archief/Speeches2019/dnb385982.jsp
14. https://www.cepweb.org/wp-content/uploads/2017/12/Klaas-Knot-speech.pdf
15. https://www.dnb.nl/en/binaries/Waterproof_tcm47-363851.pdf?2017110615
16. https://www.dnb.nl/over-dnb/samenwerking/platform-voor-duurzame-financiering/index.jsp
17. https://www.klimaatakkoord.nl/documenten/publicaties/2019/06/28/klimaatakkoord
18. https://www.dnb.nl/binaries/Special%20Committee%20on%20the%20Climate%20Crisis_tcm46-385981.pdf
19. https://www.dnb.nl/en/binaries/Values%20at%20Risk%20-%20Sustainability%20Risks%20and%20Goals%20in%20the%20Dutch_tcm47-381617.pdf
20. https://www.dnb.nl/binaries/Special%20Committee%20on%20the%20Climate%20Crisis_tcm46-385981.pdf
21. https://www.dnb.nl/binaries/Speech%202_tcm46-366089.pdf?2017112311
22. https://www.dnb.nl/en/binaries/Annual-report-DNB-2018_tcm47-382987.pdf
23. https://www.dnb.nl/binaries/Speech%202_tcm46-366089.pdf?2017112311
24. https://www.handelsblatt.com/downloads/23747594/3/hb-business_briefing_investments_12_18.pdf

25. https://publications.banque-france.fr/sites/default/files/media/2019/03/12/charte_ir_bdf_vf.pdf
26. https://www.fsb-tcfd.org/
27. https://publications.banque-france.fr/sites/default/files/media/2019/03/12/rapport-investissement-responsable-banque-france-2018-20190312_0.pdf
28. https://www.nbim.no/en/publications/reports/2018/responsible-investment-2018/
29. https://www.nbim.no/en/the-fund/news-list/2018/asset-manager-perspective-on-the-sustainable-development-goals/
30. https://www.nbim.no/contentassets/092e192d14d34d8eaf6110b75a27977c/nbim_amp_1_18_the-sdgs-and-the-gpfg.pdf
31. https://www.riksbank.se/en-gb/press-and-published/speeches-and-presentations/2019/floden-riksbank-selling-bonds-for-climate-reasons/
32. https://www.dnb.nl/binaries/Special%20Committee%20on%20the%20Climate%20Crisis_tcm46-385981.pdf
33. https://www.handelsblatt.com/downloads/21167578/6/hb-buisiness-briefing-investments_04_18.pdf
34. https://www.bundesbank.de/resource/blob/811908/9cd1506d84c6893eb5142267bde70521/mL/2019–10-monatsbericht-data.pdf
35. Sylvie Goulard & Sabine Mauderer: „Mit gutem Beispiel vorangehen“, in: Süddeutsche Zeitung, 8.7.2019
36. https://www.bundesbank.de/de/presse/reden/zentralbanken-als-klimafeuerwehr%2D%2D812426
37. https://www.bundesbank.de/de/aufgaben/themen/weidmann-und-mauderer-klimaschutz-ist-fuer-notenbanken-sehr-bedeutendes-thema%2D%2D812586
38. https://www.snb.ch/de/mmr/reference/snb_legal_richtlinien/source/snb_legal_richtlinien.de.pdf
39. https://www.luzernerzeitung.ch/wirtschaft/umweltfreundliche-investments-es-gruent-noch-wenig-bei-der-snb-ld.1078741
40. https://www.luzernerzeitung.ch/wirtschaft/klimavertraeglichkeit-nationalbank-baut-problem-engagements-nicht-ab-ld.1094648?reduced=true
41. http://www.artisansdelatransition.org/rapports/carbon-invest-schweizer-nationalbank.pdf
42. https://uploads.strikinglycdn.com/files/5a167844-9010-4efc-b3f9-6303c7d68e74/KlimaAllianz_SNB-Empfehlungen_2018-04.pdf
43. https://www.snb.ch/de/iabout/internat/multilateral/id/internat_multilateral_ngfs
44. http://ieefa.org/wp-content/uploads/2017/08/How-Renewable-Energy-Holdings-Can-Contribute-to-the-Growth-of-Norways-Pension-Fund-in-a-Time-of-Oil-Industry-Uncertainty-August-2017.pdf
45. https://www.handelsblatt.com/downloads/21167578/6/hb-buisiness-briefing-investments_04_18.pdf
46. https://www.regjeringen.no/en/aktuelt/expert-group-to-review-energy-stocks-in-the-gfpg/id2589518/
47. https://www.regjeringen.no/en/aktuelt/consultation-of-the-report-on-energy-stocks-in-the-norwegian-government-pension-fund-global/id2612615/, Press Contacts: kommunikasjonsenheten@fin.dep.no
48. https://www.nbim.no/en/publications/reports/2018/responsible-investment-2018/
49. https://www.centralbank.ie/docs/default-source/publications/economic-letters/vol-2019-no-1-climate-change-and-the-irish-financial-system-(lane).pdf?sfvrsn=8
50. https://www.ngfs.net/en
51. https://www.ecb.europa.eu/press/key/date/2018/html/ecb.sp181108.en.html
52. https://www.banque-france.fr/sites/default/files/media/2018/10/11/818366-ngfs-first-progress-report-20181011.pdf
53. https://www.banque-france.fr/sites/default/files/media/2019/04/17/ngfs_first_comprehensive_report_-_17042019_0.pdf

54. https://www.dnb.nl/en/binaries/ngfs-a-sustainable-and-responsible-investment-guide_tcm47-385934.pdf
55. https://www.ecb.europa.eu/ecb/orga/climate/html/index.de.html
56. https://www.ipbes.net/global-assessment-report-biodiversity-ecosystem-services
57. https://www.handelsblatt.com/downloads/21167578/6/hb-business-briefing-investments_04_18.pdf
58. http://www.lse.ac.uk/GranthamInstitute/publication/the-climate-impact-of-quantitative-easing/
59. http://www.wirtschaftsethik.biz/publikationen/verpflichtung-der-europaeischen-zentralbank-auf-eu-grundrechtscharta-19092017/
60. https://www.ecb.europa.eu/press/key/date/2018/html/ecb.sp181108.en.html
61. https://ec.europa.eu/info/publications/180308-action-plan-sustainable-growth_en
62. Susanne Bergius: „EU: Sustainable Finance auf dem Abstellgleis?", in: Handelsblatt Business Briefing Nachhaltige Investments, 11.10.2019 https://www.handelsblatt.com/downloads/25095704/2/hb-business-briefing-investments_10_19.pdf
63. https://ec.europa.eu/info/sites/info/files/business_economy_euro/banking_and_finance/documents/191018-international-platform-sustainable-finance-joint-statement_en.pdf
64. https://www.handelsblatt.com/downloads/21167578/6/hb-buisiness-briefing-investments_04_18.pdf
65. https://www.nachhaltigkeitsrat.de/wp-content/uploads/2019/10/2019-10-15_Stellungnahme_Sustainable_Finance_Strategie_der_Bundesregierung.pdf
66. https://www.nbim.no/contentassets/f69882edadf24bf583ac77e4307cfa8a/pri-2019-signatory-survey.pdf
67. https://www.unpri.org/about-the-pri/a-blueprint-for-responsible-investment/478.article
68. https://www.nbim.no/en/publications/consultations/2019/pri-reporting-framework-review/
69. Susanne Bergius: Nachhaltige Parallelwährung als Problemlöser" – Interview mit Stefan Brunnhuber im Tagesspiegel Background Energie & Klima, 1.10.2019

Susanne Bergius has been a freelance journalist and moderator for sustainable business and finance in Berlin since 2004 after serving 14 years as a foreign correspondent for the *Handelsblatt*. She has been the author of the column "Handelsblatt Business Briefing Nachhaltige Investments" for more than 11 years and published a handbook entitled "Geldanlagen und Investoren hinterfragen" (https://www.riffreporter.de/netzwerk-weitblick/nachhaltig_investieren/) (Scrutinize investments and investors) in 2018. She has received several awards for her work. Contact: kontakt@susanne-bergius.de

Appendices

Appendix A

08.05.2017

Offene Petition an das Europäische Parlament: **Die Europäische Zentralbank kann durch operative Ausgestaltung ihrer Mindestreserveinstrumente mitverantwortlich sein für Verstöße gegen die Charta der Grundrechte der Europäischen Union**

Mit der Bitte um Stellungnahme und Regulierung, so dass eine indirekte Beteiligung an Verstößen gegen die Charta der Grundrechte der Europäischen Union durch die Europäische Zentralbank zukünftig sicher ausgeschlossen wird

Sehr geehrte Damen und Herren,

die Europäische Zentralbank (EZB) ist mittelbar daran beteiligt, die grundlegendsten Werte der Europäischen Union zu untergraben. Dies geschieht täglich durch den Handel von mit Verstößen gegen die Charta der Grundrechte der Europäischen Union in Verbindung zu bringenden Wertpapieren. Die Auswirkungen dieses Handelns können wegen der großen Transaktionsvolumina der EZB wesentlichen Einfluss auf die weitere Entwicklung der Europäischen Union haben.

In der aktuell praktizierten operativen Mindestreservepolitik der EZB sind grundlegendste ethische Aspekte nicht sichtbar oder nicht ausreichend zu erkennen. Zudem existiert für die Berücksichtigung solcher Aspekte keine explizite Ratingverpflichtung. Das ist für eine der wichtigsten Institutionen der europäischen Idee unangemessen und wirkt direkt gegen die politischen Bemühungen um eine menschenwürdige, umweltsensible, nachhaltige und korruptionsfreie Europäische Union.

Um diesen Missstand zu beheben, sollen mittels der öffentlichen Petition und einem im Nachgang in Gang gesetzten politischen Prozess im Europäischen Parlament die EZB und damit alle in der Europäischen Union tätigen Geschäftsbanken explizit dazu verpflichtet werden…

H. Bolsinger et al. (eds.), *The European Central Bank as a Sustainability Role Model*, Sustainable Finance, https://doi.org/10.1007/978-3-030-55450-7

1. … in ihren mindestreserverelevanten Geschäften die Einhaltung von ethischen Mindestaspekten gemäß der Charta der Grundrechte der Europäischen Union sicher zu stellen und
2. … für diese mindestreserverelevanten Geschäfte in Form eines öffentlich verfügbaren Nachhaltigkeitsratings Transparenz zu schaffen.

Für eine Institution der Europäischen Union ist es unwürdig, wenn die Einhaltung der grundlegendsten Werte der Charta der Grundrechte der Europäischen Union in ihren Geschäften weder überprüft noch formal vorausgesetzt wird, obwohl dies leicht umsetzbar wäre. Es wäre für die EZB auch heute schon sehr einfach möglich, ihre als mindestreservefähig akzeptierten Wertpapiere durch externe Nachhaltigkeitsratings zu bewerten und kontroverse Schuldtitel nicht in den für alle Geschäftsbanken zwingend erforderlichen Mindestreservegeschäften zu akzeptieren.

Um die oben beschriebenen Defizite zu belegen, füge ich eine **Analyse der aktuellen Mindestreservegeschäftspolitik der EZB vom 13.03.2017** bei, die gemäß Artikel 51 („Diese Charta gilt für die Organe und Einrichtungen der Union") ebenfalls der Charta der Grundrechte der Europäischen Union zwingend verpflichtet ist.

Exemplarisch betrachtete Aspekte sind hierbei insbesondere:

- EU Grundrechtscharta Art. 32 (1) „**Kinderarbeit** ist verboten."
- EU Grundrechtscharta Art. 37 „Ein hohes **Umweltschutz**niveau [… muss] nach dem Grundsatz der nachhaltigen Entwicklung sichergestellt werden."
- **Steuervermeidung** und **Korruption** aufgrund der aktuellen Diskussion im Europäischen Parlament rund um die Erkenntnisse aus den Panama Papers
- **Menschenrechtsverletzungen**

Nach Artikel 19 der Satzung des Europäischen Systems der Zentralbanken und der Europäischen Zentralbank verlangt die EZB, dass Kreditinstitute im Rahmen des Mindestreservesystems des Eurosystems Mindestreserven auf Konten bei den nationalen Zentralbanken unterhalten.[1] Hierfür sind Kreditinstitute verpflichtet, Wertpapiere als Sicherheit zu hinterlegen. In der von der EZB publizierten Übersicht aller als Sicherheiten akzeptierten Wertpapiere[2] (EZB-Mindestreservefähigkeitsliste) befinden sich Papiere, die mit grundlegenden Werten der Europäischen Union nicht vereinbar sind und die der Charta der Grundrechte der Europäischen Union nicht vollständig gerecht werden.

Die exemplarischen Aspekte Menschenrechtskontroversen (z.B. Kinder- oder Zwangsarbeit), kontroverses Umweltverhalten und kontroverse Wirtschaftspraktiken (z.B. Korruption & fragwürdiger Umgang mit der Steuerpflicht) wurden anhand eines aktuellen Forschungsdatensatzes der unabhängigen Nachhaltigkeitsratingagentur oekom research AG (oekom) geprüft. Sie verwendet

[1] Vgl. http://www.ecb.europa.eu und https://www.bundesbank.de

[2] Siehe jeweils tagesaktuell http://www.ecb.europa.eu/mopo/assets/assets/html/index.en.html. Im vorliegenden Fall wurde der Datensatz vom 13.03.2017 verwendet.

als Maßstab dafür, welches Verhalten in diesem Sinne als kontrovers eingestuft wird, eine Operationalisierung, die auf internationalen Konventionen und Richtlinien beruht. Für die Bewertung und Einstufung der Schwere einzelner Sachverhalte bei Unternehmen und Staaten wird hierbei auf die Differenzierung zwischen schwerwiegenden und sehr schwerwiegenden Kontroversen abgestellt.[3]

Der Abdeckungsgrad der Ratingdaten beträgt rund 88%, so dass 26.110 der 29.552 von der EZB akzeptierten Wertpapiere einer Prüfung unterzogen werden konnten.

Die Prüfung ergab folgende alarmierenden Ergebnisse:

Art der Kontroversen	***Wertpapieranzahl in der EZB- Mindestreservefähigkeitsliste***
Schwerwiegende Kontroversen im Geschäftsgebaren bezüglich…	
Steuerzahlungen	4.751
Geldverkehr	2.023
Korruption	247
Umweltzerstörung	181
Menschenrechtsverletzungen	70
Produktion geächteter Waffen[4]	10
Schwerwiegende Kontroversen im Geschäftsgebaren von Zulieferern/Finanziers bezüglich…	
Menschenrechtsverletzungen	8
Kinderarbeit, Zwangsarbeit	7

Exemplarische Beispiele für gefundene Kontroversen im Rahmen der EZB-Mindestreservefähigkeitsliste:

Eine Beteiligung an der **Produktion geächteter Waffen** wird der Airbus Group unterstellt, zu der die Airbus Group Finance als von der EZB akzeptierter Wertpapieremittent gehört: „The company is involved in the production of nuclear weapons, which have been restricted by the Nuclear Non-Proliferation Treaty. The United Nations regards the way in which these weapons systems operate as inhumane. The deployment of banned weapons can undermine fundamental human rights such as 'the right to life, liberty and security of person', Art. 3, United Nations Universal Declaration of Human Rights. Nuclear weapons are considered as particularly controversial because of their indiscriminate effects on civilians and the disproportionate harm they cause."[5]

Umweltzerstörung ist für die Eni SpA eine Kontroverse, die ein von der EZB akzeptierter Wertpapieremittent ist: "Environmental impacts of the product

[3] Siehe http://oekom-research.com/index.php?content=kriterien für das verwendete Kriterienraster sowie http://oekom-research.com/index.php?content=country-kriterien für das verwendete Länderkriterienraster..

[4] Produzenten von nach dem Römer Statut des Internationalen Strafgerichtshofes geächteter Waffensysteme (z.B. ABC-Waffen)

[5] oekom Corporate Rating Airbus Group SE, Langversion vom 31.03.2017, S. 12

portfolio: The company's products and/or services are generally not compatible with the achievement of sustainable development goals. Comment: The company is mainly active in the production and/or refining of crude oil. It also has some minor business activities in the field of products and/or services with clear environmental benefits (e.g. biofuels, renewable energies). However, these positive impacts are outweighed by the negative environmental impacts from the company's core business activities."[6] Ebenso wird Royal Dutch Shell PLC, zu der die Shell International Finance BV als von der EZB akzeptierter Wertpapieremittent gehört, Umweltkontroversen unterstellt: "Continual major pollution due to flaring, spills and leaks in Nigeria."[7]

Verstöße im Geldverkehr bei Wells Fargo & Co als ein von der EZB akzeptierter Wertpapieremittent werden öffentlich diskutiert: "Business Malpractice: 2017: USD 295m in settlements related to unauthorised opening of accounts, US." [8], "According to the US Consumer Financial Protection Bureau (CFPB) in September 2016, Wells Fargo will pay USD 185 million to settle accusations that between 2011 and 2016 its employees attempted to meet high sales targets set by the company as well as to earn additional compensation by unlawfully opening around 1.5 million unauthorised accounts for customers without their knowledge."[9]

Anheuser-Busch InBev SA/NV als ein von der EZB akzeptierter Wertpapieremittent wurde im Zusammenhang mit Vorwürfen zu **Korruption** öffentlich bekannt: „2016: USD 6m settlement with US Securities and Exchange Commission for corruption charges in India."[10] Ebenso JPMorgan Chase & Co als ein von der EZB akzeptierter Wertpapieremittent: "In November 2016, JPMorgan Chase reached a settlement with the Securities and Exchange Commission (SEC) and the Department of Justice (DoJ) to resolve the allegations of hiring relatives and friends of Chinese officials in exchange for profitable business deals, thereby violating the Foreign Corrupt Practices Act."[11]

Hinweise zu möglicher Beteiligung an **Menschenrechtsverletzungen** finden sich über LafargeHolcim Ltd mit der die Holcim Finance (Luxembg) S.A. als von der EZB akzeptierter Wertpapieremittent verbunden ist: "Media reported in June 2016 that Lafarge (before the merger with Holcim in 2015 to have become LafargeHolcim) made payment deals with the terrorist group Islamic State (IS) in 2013 through till September 2014. As reported, Lafarge was accused of purchasing licenses from and paying taxes to the jihadist group through IS middlemen and oil traders to continue production at its Jalabiya cement factory in 2013, when ISIS started taking control over the city. Allegedly, the headquarter was aware of such arrangements. The company did not comment on the allegations, saying only that safety and security of its employees is its priority."[12] Kontroversen zu möglichen

[6] oekom Corporate Rating Eni SpA, Langversion vom 22.03.2017, S. 29

[7] oekom Corporate Rating Royal Dutch Shell PLC, Langversion vom 22.03.2017, S. 3

[8] oekom Corporate Rating Wells Fargo & Co, Langversion vom 10.04.2017, S. 3

[9] oekom Corporate Rating Wells Fargo & Co, Langversion vom 10.04.2017, S. 20

[10] oekom Corporate Rating Anheuser-Busch InBev SA/NV, Langversion vom 2.03.2017, S. 3 und 27

[11] oekom Corporate Rating JPMorgan Chase & Co, Langversion vom 20.03.2017, S. 25

[12] oekom Corporate Rating LafargeHolcim Ltd, Langversion vom 13.03.2017, S. 15

Menschenrechtsverletzungen werden über die International Finance Corporation als von der EZB akzeptierter Wertpapieremittent diskutiert: “2013: Major human rights violations related to palm oil producer Corporacion Dinant in Honduras.”[13] Ebenso bei Ferrovial SA mit der die Ferrovial Emisiones, S.A. als von der EZB akzeptierter Wertpapieremittent verbunden ist: “In May 2016, Ferrovial took over the Australian company Broadspectrum (previously called Transfield Services). Broadspectrum has been the lead contractor managing Australia's offshore detention centres for asylum seekers in Nauru since September 2012 and Papua New Guinea since February 2014. In June 2016, the camps hosted 442 and 854 people, respectively. The Australian government's policy of keeping refugees in foreign detention centres and the conditions in the camps have been widely and repeatedly criticised by the international community, including several bodies of the United Nations, the Australian Human Rights Commission and several NGOs. Additionally, in April 2016, Papua New Guinea's supreme court ruled that the centre in the country was unlawful and the country's government said it would shut it. In August 2016, 'The Nauru Files', a report published by the Guardian based on more than 2,000 leaked incidence reports from the camps, again shed light on numerous allegations regarding assaults, sexual abuse, self-harm attempts and bad living conditions. More than half of the reports involved children. Previously, allegations of misconduct had also been raised against some staff members of the service providers in the camp. Before the take-over, Ferrovial had indicated that the services in the detention centres were not a core part of the acquisition rationale and that it would not renew the contracts after they expire in February 2017. In response to the Nauru Files, Broadspectrum stated that it would take all allegations extremely seriously and that it had appropriately dealt with the allegations in accordance with the reporting system it has in place.”[14]

Insgesamt sind in der EZB-Mindestreservefähigkeitsliste auf Basis des Forschungsdatensatzes der oekom eine Vielzahl von fragwürdigen Wertpapieren zu finden (siehe Anlage).

Die Ergebnisse belegen, dass eine systematische Überprüfung der EZB-Mindestreservefähigkeitsliste auf ethische Aspekte hin angezeigt ist und die **EZB zukünftig regulatorisch verpflichtet werden muss, nur noch Wertpapiere zur Mindestreserve zu akzeptieren, die den ethischen Mindeststandards der Charta der Grundrechte der Europäischen Union nachweislich nicht widersprechen.**

Mit den besten Grüßen,
Harald J. Bolsinger

Verteiler:
Europäisches Parlament (Petitionsausschuss)
Politische Parteien im Europäischen Parlament
Presse
Anlage

[13] oekom Corporate Rating International Finance Corporation, Langversion vom 13.03.2017, S. 3

[14] oekom Corporate Rating Ferrovial SA, Langversion vom 16.12.2016, S. 15

Ausgewählte Nachhaltigkeitsaspekte der von der EZB am 13.03.2017 zu Mindestreservezwecken akzeptierten Wertpapiere

Eine Untersuchung des Würzburger Wirtschaftsethikers Harald J. Bolsinger. Datenstand: oekom 30.3.2017, EZB 13.03.2017. Eine Anforderung des Forschungsdatensatzes seitens der Politik, um die Analyse kleinteilig nachprüfen zu können, ist direkt bei der oekom research AG möglich.		Controverse Activities									
		Business Malpractice - Company: Taxes	Business Malpractice - Company: Corruption	Business Malpractice - Company: Money transfers	Controversial Environmental Practices - Company	Human Rights	Human Rights Controversies - Company	Human Rights Controversies - Financiers	Labour Rights Controversies - Supplier: Child labour	Labour Rights Controversies - Supplier: Forced labour	Military - Producer: weapons (systems) – banned
	Financials/Commercial Banks & Capital Markets	3.033	39	2.020							
	Financials/Public & Regional Banks	1.693									
	Oil, Gas & Consumable Fuels		48		106		29				
	Food & Beverages		75						7	7	
	Utilities		38		31		31				
	Automobile				32						
	Transport & Logistics/Rail		28								
	Tobacco	22									
	Pharmaceuticals & Biotechnology		15								
	Aerospace & Defence										8
	Construction Materials				8		8				
	Financials/Development Banks							8			
	Machinery		4								
	Insurance	3		3							
	Metals & Mining				3						
	Commercial Services & Supplies										2
	Construction						2				
	Oil & Gas Equipment/Services				1						
Industry	TOTAL	4.751	247	2.023	181		70	8	7	7	10
	DE	2.462	28	576	32						
	FR	1.582	4	466	14						3
	IT	397	61	361	28						
	GB	106	31	242	41		20				2
	SE			202							
	US		39	109				8			
	ES	91	2		40		42				
	CH	90	4	66	8		8		7	7	
	BE		75								
	CA	23									
	NO				17						
	NL										5
	HU					4					
	LV		3								
	CW				1						
	JP			1							
Country	TOTAL	4.751	247	2.023	181	4	70	8	7	7	10
	Listed corporate	2.503	216	2.023	181		70		7	7	10
	Non-listed corporate	2.248	31					8			
	Sovereign					4					
Issuer Category	**TOTAL**	**4.751**	**247**	**2.023**	**181**	**4**	**70**	**8**	**7**	**7**	**10**

Appendix B

Translation of the document transmitted on 04.01.2018 in German language

Summary and update of petition 0429/2017 to the European Parliament: European Central Bank (ECB) involved in a massive number of violations of the Charter of Fundamental Rights of the European Union through possession and trading of unethical securities.

Ladies and gentlemen,

you were asked by the European Parliament's Committee on Petition 0429/2017 for an opinion. To make this easier for you, I have summarized the facts and attached an update of my study[15]:

Circumstances

The ECB is playing a major role in undermining the most fundamental values of the European Union by accepting questionable securities as collateral for its monetary policy operations. The effects of this action have a significant influence on the development of the European Union due to its large transaction volume. Therefore, the ECB and its agents must refrain from trading in and holding securities related to infringements of the Charter of Fundamental Rights of the European Union.

4781 Banks and savings banks were obliged in the euro area in 2017 to hold minimum reserve assets with the ECB (or its national central bank). A further 2493 financial institutions and funds were listed business partners of the ECB for refinancing operations. This meant that 7274 banks, savings banks, money market funds and financial institutions, including national central banks, were obliged to hold so-called eligible collateral for monetary policy transactions with the ECB in their portfolios. The traded volume of these securities currently stands at around €14 trillion and is thus a major lever for or against the realisation of European values in the real economy. The ECB (or the respective national central bank as vicarious agent) becomes the owner of the relevant securities as a pledgee eligible collateral. Trade in and possession of securities which undermine the Charter of Fundamental Rights of the European Union is detrimental to the European Union. For a European institution such as the ECB, this is unacceptable and cannot be justified by independence in monetary policy.[16]

[15] http://www.wirtschaftsethik.biz/zentralbank

[16] In accordance with Article 51 the ECB is bound by and not above the Charter of Fundamental Rights of the European Union.

Supporting Documents

The ECB's website provides access to its daily updated list of marketable collateral accepted as collateral for monetary policy operations (= marketable eligible collateral). In addition, there are also unpublished, non-marketable securities that meet the eligibility criteria and are accepted as collateral. The marketable securities of all issuers meeting the central bank eligibility criteria on January 3, 2018 were examined by the independent sustainability rating agency oekom research AG (oekom) on January 4, 2018 with daily ratings. Of the 29,445 securities, 25,111 were examined with daily ratings, which corresponds to a coverage ratio of 85%. Once again, the investigation focused only on serious and very serious ethical controversies of the aspects of the EU Charter of Fundamental Rights, which were examined in 2017 (Article 32 Child Labour; Article 37 Environmental Protection; Article 5 Violations of human rights, such as forced labour; tax avoidance and corruption). The audit again revealed the following alarming results (and thus an increase in infringements):

Type of controversy	*Number of securities in the ECB register of marketable collateral*
Serious controversies in business conduct regarding...	
• Tax payments	4481 securities
• Cash transactions	1592 securities
• Corruption	936 securities
• Environmental protection	1.480 securities
• Human rights violations	72 securities
• Production of outlawed weapons	16 securities

Remedy

In order to remedy the deplorable state of affairs simply and effectively, the permanent non-infringement of the EU Charter of Fundamental Rights must be included in the criteria for eligible collateral as a condition for admission. Compliance with the EU Charter of Fundamental Rights is regularly verified by a current ethical rating. In terms of competition policy, the ethical rating can be transparently mapped by means of the independent ethical ratings already available on the market from established rating agencies to which the ECB and all other financial market players have access at all times.

Reasons

The existence of the EU Charter of Fundamental Rights implies a natural obligation for the ECB to proceed as proposed above. Since my analysis of marketable central bank eligible collateral has revealed mass violations of the Charter of Fundamental

Rights of the European Union, explicit inclusion of this European minimum morality in the ECB's statutes is urgently needed. To date, the ECB and the European financial market have not been sufficient to enforce the Charter of Fundamental Rights of the European Union.

Sincerely,

Harald J. Bolsinger